Aristotle

Aristotle's Master-Piece Completed

The First Containing the Secrets of Generation in all the Parts Thereof -

The Second Part Being A Private Looking-Glass for the Female Sex

Aristotle

Aristotle's Master-Piece Completed
The First Containing the Secrets of Generation in all the Parts Thereof - The Second Part Being A Private Looking-Glass for the Female Sex

ISBN/EAN: 9783337250362

Printed in Europe, USA, Canada, Australia, Japan

Cover: Foto ©ninafisch / pixelio.de

More available books at **www.hansebooks.com**

The Effigies of a Maid all hairy and an Infant that was born black by the Imagination of the Parents.

IN TWO PARTS.

The First containing the Secrets of Generation in all the Parts thereof.

TREATING

Of the Benefit of Marriage, and the Prejudice of unequal Matches, Signs of Insufficiency in Men or Women. Of the infusion of the Soul. Of the Likeness of Children to Parents. Of Monstrous Births. The Cause and Cure of the Green Sickness, a Discourse of Virginity. Directions and Cautions for Midwives. Of the Organs of Generation in Women, and the Fabric of the Womb. The Use and Action of the Genitals. Signs of Conception, and whether a Male or Female; with a Word of Advice to both Sexes in the Act of Copulation. And the Picture of several Monstrous Births, &c.

THE SECOND PART BEING

A Private Looking-Glass for the Female Sex.

Treating of the various Maladies of the Womb, and all other Distempers incident to Women of all Ages, with proper Remedies for the Cure of each. The whole being more Correct than any Thing of this Kind hitherto Published.

NEW-YORK:
PRINTED FOR THE COMPANY OF FLYING STATIONERS. 1793.

INTRODUCTION.

IF one of the meaneſt capacity were aſked, What was the wonder of the world? I think the moſt proper anſwer would be, MAN: He being the little world to whom all things are ſubordinate; agreeing in the genius with ſenſitive things; all being animals, but differing in the ſpecies. For man alone is endowed with reaſon.

And therefore the Deity at man's creation (as the inſpired penman tells us) ſaid, "Let us make man "in our own image, that he may be (as a creature "may be) like Us, and the ſame in his likeneſs, may "be our image:" Some of the fathers do diſtinguiſh, as if by the image the Lord doth plant the reaſonable powers of the ſoul, reaſon, will and memory; and by likeneſs, the qualities of the mind, charity, juſtice, patience, &c. But Moſes confounded this diſtinction, (if you compare theſe texts of ſcripture) Gen. i. 17. and v. 1 Coloſſ. x. Eph. v. 14. And the apoſtle where he ſaith, "He was created "after the image of God, knowledge, and the ſame "in righteouſneſs and holineſs." The Greeks there repreſent him, as one turning his eyes upwards towards him, whoſe image and ſuperſcription he bears.

See how the heaven's high Architect
 Hath fram'd him in this wiſe,
To ſtand, to go, to look erect,
 With body, face, and eyes.

And Cicero ſays, like Moſes, all creatures were made to rot on the earth except man, to whom was given an upright frame to contemplate his Maker, and behold the manſion prepared for him above.

Now to the end that so noble and glorious a creature might not quite perish, it pleased God to give unto woman the field of generation for a recepticle of human seed, whereby that natural and vegitable soul, which lies potentially in the seed, may, by the plastic power be reduced into act; that man, who is a mortal creature, by leaving his offspring behind him, may become immortal, and survive in his posterity.

And because this field of generation, the womb, is the place where this excellent creature is formed, and that in so wonderful a manner, that the Royal Psalmist (having meditated thereon) cries out as one in ecstasy, "I am fearfully and wonderfully made." It will be necessary to treat largely thereon in this book which, to that end, is divided into two parts: The first whereof treats of the manner and parts of generation in both sexes; for from the mutual desire they have to each other, which nature has implanted in them to that end, that delight which they take in the act of copulation, does the whole race of mankind proceed; and a particular account of what things are previous to that act, and also what are consequential of it, and how each member concerned in it is adapted and fitted to that work, to which nature has designed it. And though in uttering of those things, something may be said, which those that are unclean may make bad use of, and use it as a motive to stir up their bestial appetites; yet such may know that this was never intended for them, nor do I know any reason that those sober persons for whose use this was meant, should want the help hereby designed them, because vain loose persons will be ready to abuse it.

The second part of this treatise is wholly designed for the female sex, and does largely not only treat of the destempers of the womb, and the various causes, but also give you proper remedies for the cure of them; for such is the ignorance of most women, that when, by any distemper, those parts are affected, they neither know from whence it proceeds, nor how to apply a remedy; and such is their modesty also, that they are unwilling to ask, that they may be informed; and for the help of such this is designed, for having my being from a woman, I thought none had more right to the grapes than she that planted the vine.

And therefore observing that among all diseases incident to the body, there are none more frequent and perilous, than those that do arise from the ill state of the womb, for through the evil quality thereof, the heart, the liver, and the brain are affected, from whence the actions, vital, natural, and animal, are hurt, and the virtues concoctive, sanguinificative, distributive, attractive, expulsive, retentive, with the rest, are all weakened, so that from the womb, come convulsions, epilepsies, apoplexies, palsies and fevers, dropsies, malignant ulcers, &c. And there is no disease so bad, but may grow worse from the evil quality of it.

How necessary therefore is the knowledge of these things let every unprejudiced reader judge, for that many women labor under them, through their ignorance and modesty (as I said before) woful experience makes manifest; here, therefore, (as in a mirror) they may be acquainted with their own distempers, and have suitable remedies, without applying themselves to physicians, against which they have so great reluctance.

A 2

ARISTOTLE's MASTER-PIECE COMPLETED.

PART FIRST.

CHAP. I.

Of Marriage, and at what Age Young Men and Virgins are capable of it; and why they so much desire it; also how long Men and Women are capable of having Children.

THERE are very few (except some profest debauchees) but what will readily agree, that marriage is honorable to all, being ordained by heaven in Paradise, and without which no man or woman can be in a capacity honestly to yield obedience to the first law of the creation—increase and multiply: and since it is natural in young people to desire these mutual embraces, proper to the marriage-bed, it behoves parents to look after their children, and when they find them inclinable to marriage, not violently to restrain their affections, and oppose their inclinations, (which, instead of allaying them, makes them but the more impetuous) but rather provide such suitable matches for them, as may make their lives comfortable, lest the crossing of their inclinations should precipitate them to commit those follies that may bring an indeliable stain upon their families.

The inclinations of maids to marriage, is to be known by many symptoms, for when they arrive at puberty, which is about the fourteenth or fifteenth year of their age, then their natural purgations begin to flow, and the blood which is no longer taken to augment their bodies, abounding, stirs up their minds to venery: External causes also may incite them to it, for their spirits being brisk and enflamed when they arrive at this age, if they eat hard salt things, and spices, the body becomes more and more heated, whereby the desire to venereal embraces is very great, and sometimes almost insuperable. And the use of this so much desired employment being denied, to virgins many times is followed by dismal consequences, as a green weasel colour, short breathings, trembling of the heart, &c. But when they are married, and their venereal desires satisfied by the enjoyment of their husbands, those distempers vanish, and they become more gay and lively than before; also their eager staring at men, and affecting their company, shews that nature pushes them upon coition, and their parents neglecting to get them husbands, they break through modesty to satisfy themselves in unlawful embraces; it is the same in brisk widows, who cannot be satisfied without the benevolence which their husbands used to give them.

At the age of fourteen the menses in girls begin to flow, when they are capable of conceiving, and continue generally to forty-four, when they cease bearing, unless their bodies are strong and healthful, which sometimes enables them to bear at fifty-five. But many times the menses proceed from some violence offered to nature, or some morbific matter which often proves fatal to the party, and therefore those men that are desirous of issue, must marry a woman within the age aforesaid, or blame themselves if they meet with disappointments: Though, if an old man not worn out by diseases and incontinency, marry a brisk lively lass, there is hopes of his having children to three score and ten, nay, sometimes till four score.

Hippocrates holds, that a youth at fifteen years, or between that and seventeen, having much vital strength, is capable of getting children; and also, that the force of procreating matter increases till forty-five, fifty, and fifty-five, and then begins to flag, the seeds by degrees becoming unfruitful, the natural spirits being extinguished, and the humours dried up. Thus in general, but as to particulars, it often falls out otherwise: nay, it is reported by a credible author, that in Swedland, a man was married at one hundred years, to a bride of thirty, and had many children by her, but his countenance was so fresh, that those that knew him not, took him not to exceed fifty. And in Campania, where the air is clear and temperate, men of eighty years old, marry young virgins, and has children by them; shewing that age in them hinders not procreation unless they be exhausted in their youth, and their yards shriveled up.

If any would know why a woman is sooner barren than a man, they may be assured, that the natural heat, which is the cause of generation, is more predominant in the latter than in the former: for since a woman is truly more moist than a man, as her monthly purgations demonstrate, as also the softness of her body; it is also apparent, that he doth not exceed her in natural heat, which is the chief things that concocts the humours into proper aliment, which the woman wanting, grows fat; when a man, through his native heat, melts his fat by degrees, and his humours are dissolved, and by the benefit thereof are elaborated into seed. And this may also be added that women generally are not so strong as men, nor so wise nor prudent, nor have so much reason and ingenuity in ordering affairs, which shews that thereby their faculties are hindered in operations.

CHAP. II.

How to get a Male or Female Child, and of the Embryo and perfect Birth, and the fittest Time for Copulation.

WHEN a young couple are married, they naturally desire children, and therefore use those means that nature has appointed to that end; but notwithstanding their endeavors, they must know the success of all depends on a blessing of the Lord; not only so, but the sex, whether male or female, is from his disposal also; though it cannot be denied, but secondary causes have influence therein, especially two——First, The genteial humour, which is brought by the arteria præparaentes to the testes in form of blood, and there elaborated into seed by the seminifical faculty residing in them; to which may be added the desire of coition, which fires the imagination with unusual fancies, and by the sight of brisk charming beauty, may soon inflame the appetite; but if nature be enfeebled, such meats must be eaten as will conduce to the affording such aliment as makes the seed abound and restores the decays of nature, that the faculties may freely operate, and remove impediments obstructing the procreation of children.

Then since diet alters the evil state of the body to a better, those who are subject to barrenness must eat such meats as are of good juice, that nourish well, making the body lively and full of sap, of which faculty are all hot moist meats: For, according to Galen, seed is made of pure concocted and windy superfluity of blood, where we may conclude there is a power in many things to accummulate seed, also to augment it, and other things of force to cause erection, as hen eggs, pheasants, woodcocks, gnatsnappers, thrushes, blackbirds, young pigeons, sparrows, partridges, capons, almonds, pine nuts, raisins, currants, all strong wines taken sparingly, especially those made of the grapes of Italy; but erection is chiefly caused by scuram, eringoes, cresses, erysmon, parsnips, artichokes, turnips, rapes, asparagus, candied ginger, galings, acorns bruised to powder drank in muscadel, scallion, sea shellfish, &c.—but these must have time to perform their operation, and must use them for a considerable time, or you will reap but little benefit by them. The act of coition being over, let the woman repose herself on her right side, with her head lying low, and her body declining, that by sleeping in that posture, the cawl on the right side of the matrix may prove the place of the conception, for therein is the greatest generative heat, which is the chief procuring cause of male children, and rarely fails the expectation of those that experience it, especially if they do but keep warm without much motion, leaning to the right, and drinking a little spirit of saffron and juice of hysop in a glass of malaga or alicant, when they lie down and arise, for the space of a week.

For a female child, let a woman lie on the left side, strongly fancying a female in the time of procreation, drinking the decoction of female mercury four days from the first day of purgation—the male mercury having the like operation in case of a male; for this concoction purges the right and left side of the womb, opens the receptacles, and makes way for the seminary of generation to beget a female, the best time is, when the moon is in the wane, in Libra or Acqurrus. Advicene says, "When the menses " are spent, and the womb cleansed, which is com- " monly in five or seven days at most, if a man lie " with his wife from the first day she is purged to

"the fifth, she will conceive a male, but from the
"fifth to the eighth a female, and from the eighth to
"the twelfth a male again; but after that perhaps
"neither distinctly, but both in a hermaphrodite."
In a word, they that would be happy in the fruits of
their labor, must observe to use copulation in due
distance of time, not too often nor too seldom, for
both are alike hurtful; and to use it immediately
weakens and wastes their spirits, and spoils the
seed; and thus much for the first particular. The
second is to let the reader know how the child is
formed in the womb, what accident it is liable to
there, how nourished and brought forth.

There are various opinions concerning this matter; therefore I will shew what the learned say about it. Man consists of an egg, which is impregnated in the testicles of the woman, by the more subtle part of the man's seed. but the forming faculty and virtue in the seed is a divine gift, it being abundantly endued with a vital spirit, which gives sap and form to the embryo: so that all parts and bulk of the body, which is made up in a few months, and gradually formed into the lovely figure of a man, do consist in, and are adumbrated thereby, which is incomparably expressed in the cxxxix. Psalm, "I will praise thee, O Lord, because I am "wonderfully made, &c." And the physicians have slighted four different times, wherein a man is framed and perfected in the womb, the first moon after coition being perfected in the first week, if no flux happens, which sometimes falls out, through the slipperness of the matrix of the head thereof, that shuts over like a rose bud, and opens on a sudden by means of forming, is affirmed to be when nature makes manifest mutation in the conception, so that all the substance seems congealed flesh and blood, which happens twelve or fourteen days after copulation. And though this fleshy mass abounds with fiery blood, yet it remains undistinguishable, without form or figure, and may be called an embryo, and compared to seed sown in the ground, which, through heat and moisture, grows by degrees into a perfect form, either in plant or grain. The third time assigned to make up this fabric is when the principal parts shew themselves plain, as the heart whence proceed the arteries. The brain from which the nerves, like small threads, run through the whole body, and the liver, that divides the chyle from the blood brought to it by the venna porta, the two first are fountains of life that nourish every part of the body, in framing which, the faculty of the womb is buried from the time of conception to the eighth day of the first month.

Lastly—About the thirtieth day the outward parts are seen finely wrought, and distinguished by joints, when the child begins to grow, from which time, by reason the limbs are divided, and the whole frame is perfect, it is no longer an embryo but a perfect child. Most males are perfect by the thirtieth day, but females seldom to the forty-second or forty-fifth day, because the heat of the womb is greater in producing the male than the female; and for the same reason a woman going with a male child quickens in three months, but going with a female rarely under four, at which time also its hair and nails come forth, and the child begins to stir, kick, and move in the womb, and then women are troubled with loathing of their meat, and greedy longing for things contrary to nutriment, as coals, rubbish, chalk &c. which desire often occasions abortion, and miscarriage. Some women have been so extravagant as to long for hob-nails, leather, mens flesh, horse flesh, and other unnatural as well as unwholesome food, for want of which things they have either miscarried, or the child has continued dead in the womb for several days, to the imminent hazard of their lives. But I shall now proceed to shew by what real means the infant is sustained in the womb, and what posture it their remains in.

Various are the opinions about nourishing the fœtus in the womb; some say by blood only, from the umbilical vein, others by the chyle, taken in by the mouth; but it is nourished diversly according to the several degrees of perfection, that an egg passes from a conception to a fœtus ready for birth. But first, let us explain the meaning of the ovum or egg: In the generation of the fœtus there are two principals active and passive—the active is the man's seed elaborated in the testicles, out of arterial blood and animal spirits—the passive is an egg impregnated by the man's seed. And the nature of conception is thus: The most spirituous part of the man's seed, in the act of generation, reaching up to the testicles of the woman, which contains divers eggs, impregnates one of them, which being conveyed by the oviducts to the bottom of the womb, presently begins to swell bigger and bigger, and drinks in the moisture that is plentifully sent thither, as seeds suck moisture in the ground, to make them sprout out, when the parts of the embryo begin to be a little more perfect, and that at the same time the chorin is very thick, that the liquor cannot soak thro' it, the umbilical vessels begin to be formed, and to extend the side of the amnion, which they pass thro', and all through the aliantreides and chorin, and are implanted in the placenta, which gathering upon the chorin, joins to the uterus. And now the arteries that before sent out the nourishment into the cavity of the womb, open by the orifice into the placenta, where they deposite the said juice, which is drunk up by the umbilical vein, and conveyed by it, first to the liver of the fœtus, and then to the heart, where its more thin and spiritous part is turned into blood, while the grosser part descending by

Aristotle's Master-Piece completed. 15

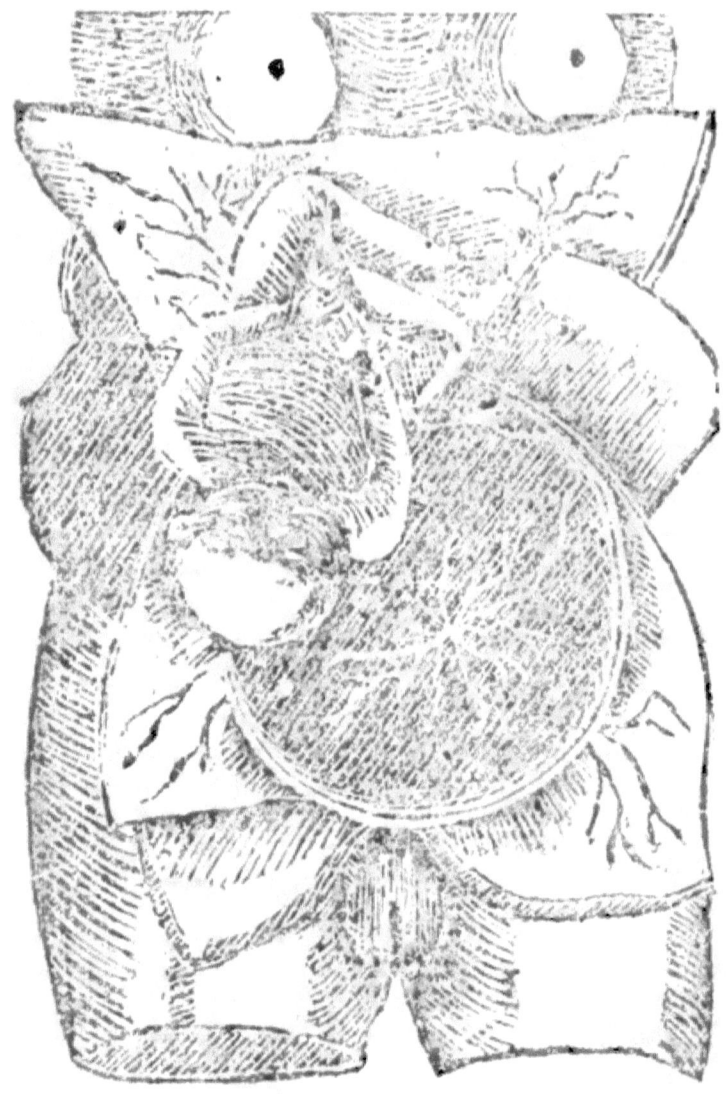

The Form of a Child in the Womb, distiched of its
Tunicles proper and common.

the aorta, enters the umbilical arteries, and is discharged into its cavity, by those branches that run through the amnion.

As soon as the mouth, stomach, gullet, &c. are formed so perfectly, that the fœtus can swallow, it sucks in some of the grosser nutricious juice, that is deposited in the amnion by the umbilical arteries, which descending into the stomach and intestines, is received by the lacteal veins, as in adult persons.

The fœtus being perfected, at the time before specified, in all its parts, it lies equally balanced in the womb, as the centre on his head, and being long turned oval, so that the head a little inclines, and it lays its chin on its breast, its heels and ancles upon its buttocks, its hands on its cheeks, and its thumbs to its eyes; but its legs and thighs are carried upwards, with its hams bending, so that they touch the bottom of its belly, the former and that part of the body which is over against us, as the forehead, nose, and face are towards the mother's back, and the head inclining downwards, towards the rump-bone, that joins to the os sacrum, which bone, together with the os pubis, in the time of birth, part is loosed, whence it is, that the male children commonly come with their faces downwards, or with their head turned somewhat oblique, that their faces may be seen, but the female children with their faces upwards, though sometimes it happens that births do not follow according to nature's order, but children come forth with their feet standing, their necks bowed, and their heads lying oblique, with their hands stretched out, which greatly endangers themselves and the mother, giving the midwife great trouble to bring them into the world; but when all things proceed in nature's order, the child when the time of birth is accomplished, is desirous to come forth of the womb, and by inclining himself he rolls downwards, for he can no more be obscured in those hidden places, and the heat of the heart cannot subsist without external respiration, whereof being grown great, more and more desirous of nutriment and light, when covering the ætherial air, by struggling to obtain it, breaks the membranes and coverings, whereby he was restrained and fenced against attrition, and for the most part with bitter pangs of the mother, issueth forth into the world commonly in the ninth month. For the matrix being divided, and the os pubis loosened, the woman strives to cast out her burden, and the child does the like to get forth, by the help of its inbred strength, and so the birth comes to be perfect; but if the child be dead, the more dangerous the delivery, though nature often helps the woman's weakness herein; but the child that is quick and lively, labors no less than the woman. Now there are births at seven or eight months, and some women go to the tenth month; but of these and the reasons of them, I shall speak more largely in another place.

CHAP. III.

The reason why Children are like their Parents, and that the Mother's Imagination contribute thereto, and whether the Man or Woman is the Cause of the Male or Female Child.

LACTANTIUS is of opinion, that when a man's seed falls on the left side of the womb; it may procure a male child; but because it is the proper place for a female, there will be something in it that resembles a woman; that is, it will be fairer, whiter, and smoother, not very subject to have hair on the body or chin; it will have lank hair on the head, the voice small and sharp, and the courage feeble: and on the contrary, that a female may chance to be gotten if the seed fall on the right side; but then, through the abundance of the heat, she shall be big boned, full of courage, having a masculine voice, and her chin and bosom hairy, not being so clear as others of that sex, and subject to quarrel with her husband for superiority.

In case of similitude, nothing is more powerful than the imagination of the mother; for if she fasten her eyes upon any object, and imprint it on her mind, it oftentimes so happens, that the child in some part or other of its body, has a representation thereof, and if in the act of copulation, the woman earnestly look upon the man, and fix her mind upon him, the child will resemble its father. Nay, though a woman in unlawful copulation, yet if she fix her mind upon her husband, the child will resemble him, though he never got it. The same effect of imagination causes warts, stains, molth-spots, dastes, though indeed they sometimes happen thro' frights or extravagant longing; many women being with child seeing a hare cross them, will, through the force of imagination, bring forth a child with a hairy lip. Some children are born with flat noses, wry mouths, great blubber lips, and ill shaped bodies: and must ascribe the reason to the imagination of the mother, who hath cast her eyes and mind upon some ill-shaped creatures: Therefore it behoves all women with child if possible, to avoid such sights or, at least, not regard them. But though the mother's imagination may contribute much to the features of the child, yet in manners, wit, and propension of the mind, experience tells us, that children are commonly of the condition with the parents, and same tempers. But the vigor or disability of persons in the act of copulation, many times causes it to be otherwise: For children got through the heat and strength of desire, must needs partake more of the nature and inclination of their parents, than those that are begotten with desires more weak: And therefore the children begotten by men in their old age, are generally weaker than those begotten by them in their youth.

As to the share which each of the parents has in begetting the child, we will give the opinion of the ancients about it.

Though it is apparent (say they) that the man's seed is the chief efficient beginning of action, motion and generation; yet that the woman affords seed, and effectually contributes in that point to the procreation of the child, is evinced by strong reasons. In the first place seminary vessels has been given her in vain, and genital testicles inverted, if the woman wanted seminal excrescence; for nature doth nothing in vain; therefore we must grant they were made for the use of seed and procreation, and fixed in their proper place, both the testicles and receptacles of seed whose nature is to operate and afford virtue to the seed. And to prove this, there needs no stronger argument (say they) than, that if a woman do not use copulation to eject her seed, she often falls into strange diseases, as appears by young women and virgins: A second reason they urge is, that although the society of a lawful bed consist not altogether in these things, yet it is apparent, the female sex are never better pleased, nor appear more blithe and jocund than when they are satisfied this way; which is an inducement to believe, they have more pleasure and titulation therein than men. For, since nature causes much delight to accompany ejection, by the breaking forth of the swelling spirits, and the swiftness of the nerves; in which case, the operation on the woman's part is double, she having in enjoyment both by ejection and reception, by which she is more delighted in the act.

Hence it is (say they) that the child more frequently resembles the mother than the father, because the mother contributes most towards it. And they think it may be further instanced, from the endeared affection they bear them; for, that besides there further instanced, from the endeared affection contributing seminal matter, they feed and nourish the child with the purest fountain of blood until its birth. Which opinion, Galen affirms, by allowing children to participate most of the mother, and ascribes the difference of sex to the operation of the menstrual blood; but the reason of the likeness he refers to the power of the seed; for, as plants receive more nourishment from fruitful ground, than from the industry of the husbandman; so the infant receives in more abundance from the mother than the father. For first, the seed of both is cherished in the womb and there grows to perfection, being nourished with blood: And for this reason it is (say they) that children for the most part love their mother best, because they receive most of their substance from their mother: For about nine months she nourishes her child in the womb, with her purest blood, then her love towards it newly born, and its likeness do clearly shew, that the woman affordeth feed, and contributes more towards making the child than the man.

But in all this the ancients are very erroneous, for the testicles (so called in women) afford not any feed but are two eggs, like those of fowls, and other creatures; neither have they any office as those of men, but are indeed ovaria, wherein the eggs are nourished by the sanguinary vessels dispersed through them, and from thence one or more (as they are fœcundated by the man's seed) is separated and conveyed into the womb by the oviducts. The truth of this is plain, for if you boil them, their liquor will be the same colour, taste and consistency, with the taste to birds eggs; if any object they have no shells, that signifies nothing; for the eggs of fowls, while they are in the ovary; nay after they are fastened to the uterus, have no shell: And though when they are laid they have one, yet that is on more than a defence which nature has provided them against any outward injury, while they are hatched without the body: whereas those of the women being hatched within the body, need no other fence than the womb, by which they are sufficiently secured.

And this is enough, I hope, for the clearing of this point. As to the third thing proposed, as whence grows the kind, and whether the man or woman is the cause of the male or female infant.

The primary cause we must ascribe to God, as is most justly his due, who is the ruler and disposer of all things, yet he suffers many things to proceed according to the rules of nature, which proceed by their inbred motion, according to usual and natural courses, without variation. Though, indeed, by favor from on high, Sarah conceived Isaac, Hannah, Samuel, and Elizabeth, John the Baptist: But these are all very extraordinary things brought to pass by a Divine Power, above the course of nature; nor have such instances been wanting in latter days; therefore I shall wave them, and proceed to speak of things natural. The ancient physicians and philosophers say, That since there are two principals out of which the body of man is made, and which render the child like the parents, and by one or the other sex, viz. Seed common to both sexes, and menstrual blood proper to the woman only, the similitude (say they) must needs consist in the force or virtue of the male or female; so that it proves like the one or the other, according to the plenty afforded by either; but that the difference of the sex is not referred to the seed, but to the menstrual blood which is proper to the women, is apparent. For were that force altogether retained in the seed, the male seed being of the hottest quality, male children would abound and few of the female be propagated; where-

B

fore the sex is attributed to the temperament of the active qualities, which consist in the heat and cold, and the nature of the matter under them; that is, the flowing of the menstruous blood; but now the seed (say they) affords both force to procreate and form the child, and matter for its generation; and in the menstruous blood there is both matter and force; for as the seed most helps the material principal, so also does the menstrual blood the potential seed; which is (says Galen) blood well concocted by the vessels that contain it. So that blood is not only the matter of generating the child, but also seed in possibility that menstrual blood hath both principals.

The ancients further say, That the seed is the stronger efficient; the matter of it being very little in quantity, but the potential quality of it is very strong: wherefore if these principals of generation, according to which the sex is made, were only (say they) in the menstrual blood then would the children be all mostly females: as, were the efficient force in the seed, they would be all males; but since both have operation in menstrual blood, matter predominates in quantity; and in the seed, force and virtue. And therefore Galen thinks the child receives its sex rather from the mother than from the father; for though his seed contribute a little to the material principle, yet it is more weakly. But for likeness it is referred rather to the father, than to the mother. Yet the woman's seed receiving strength from the menstrual blood, for the space of nine months, over-powers the man's as to that particular; for the menstrual blood flowing in the vessels, rather cherishes the one than the other; from which it is plain, the woman affords both matter to make, and force and virtue to perfect the conception; though the female's seed be fit nutriment for the male's, by reason of the thinness of it, being more adapted to make up conception thereby. For as of soft wax and moist clay, the artificer can frame what he intends, so say they, the man's seed mixing with the woman's, and also with the menstrual blood, helps to form and perfect part of man.

But with all imaginable deference to the wisdom of our fathers, give me leave to say, that their ignorance in the anatomy of man's body, has led them into the paths of error, and run them into great mistakes, for their hypothesis of the formation of the embryo from the coto-mixture of seed, and the nourishment of it too in the menstruous blood being wholly false, their opinion in this case must of necessity be so also.

I shall therefore conclude this chapter and only say, that although a strong imagination of the mother may often determine the sex, yet the main agent in this case is the plastic and formative principal, which is the efficient in giving form to the child, which gives it this or that sex, according to those laws and rules given to us by the wise Creator of all things, who both makes and fashions it, and therein determines the sex according to the counsel of his own will.

CHAP. IV.

A Discourse of Man's Soul, that it is not propagated by the Parents, but is infused by its Creator, and can neither die nor corrupt. At what Time it is infused, of its Immortality, and certainty of the Resurrection.

MAN's soul is of so divine a nature and excellency, that man himself cannot in any wise comprehend it, it being the infused breath of the Almighty, of an immortal nature, and not to be comprehended but by him that gave it. For Moses by holy inspiration, relating the original of man, tells us, "That God breathed into his nostrils the breath of life, and he became a living soul." Now as for all other creatures, at his word they were made and had life; but the creature God had appointed to set over his works, was the peculiar workmanship of the Almighty, forming him out of the dust of the earth, and condescending to breathe into his nostrils the breath of life, which seems to denote more care and (if we may so term it) labor used about man, than about all other creatures, he only partaking and participating of the blessed divine nature, bearing God's image in innocence and purity; whilst he stood firm, and when by his fall that lively image was defaced, yet such was the love of his Creator towards him, that he found out a way to restore him; the only begotten Son of the eternal Father, coming into the world to destroy the works of the devil, and to raise up man from that low condition, to which his sin and fall had reduced him, to a state above that of angels.

If therefore man would understand the excellency of his soul, let him turn his eyes inwardly and look into himself, and search diligently his own mind; and there he shall see many admirable gifts and excellent ornaments, that must needs possess him with wonder and amazement, as reason, understanding, freedom of will, memory, &c. That plainly shew the soul to be descended from a heavenly original, and that therefore it is of infinite duration, and not subject to annihilation. Yet for its many offices and operations whilst in the body, it goes under several denominations: For when it enlivens the body, it is called the soul; when it gives knowledge, the judgment or mind: and when it recals things past, the memory; whilst it discourses and discerns, reason; whilst it contemplates, the spirit; whilst it is the sensitive parts, the senses. And these are the principle offices, whereby the soul declares its power, and performs its action. for being seated in the highest parts of the body, it diffuseth its force into every member; not propagated from the parents, nor mixed with gross matter; but the infused breath of God immediately proceeding from him, not passing from one to another as was the opinion of Pythagoras who held a transmigration of the soul, but that the soul is given to every infant by infusion, is the most received and orthodox opinion; and the learned do likewise agree, that this is done when the infant is perfected in the womb, which happens about the twenty-fourth day after conception, especially for males, who are generally born at the end of nine months: but in females who are not so soon formed and perfected, through defect of heat, not till the fiftieth day. And though this day in all cases cannot be truly set down, yet Hippocrates has given his opinion, when the child has its present form, when it begins to move, and when born if in due season: In this book of the nature of infants, he says, if it be a male, and he be perfect on the thirtieth day, and move on the nintieth day he will be born on the seventh month; but if he be perfectly formed on the thirty-fifth day, he will move on the seventieth, and be born on the eighth month. Again if he be perfectly formed on the fifty fifth day he will move on the nintieth, and be born in the ninth month. Now from those passing of days and months, it plainly appears, that the day of forming being doubled, makes up the day of moving, and that day three times reckoned, makes up the day of birth.

As thus, when thirty-five perfects the form, if you double it, makes seventy, the day of motion, and three times seventy, amount to two hundred and ten days, which allowing thirty days to a month, makes seven months; and so you must consider the rest. But as to a female, the case is different, for it is longer perfecting in the womb, the mother ever going longer with a boy than a girl, which makes the account differ; for a female formed in thirty days, moves not till the seventieth day, and is born in the eighth month; when she is formed on the fortieth, she moves not till the eightieth, and is born on the eighth month; but if she be perfectly formed on the fifty-fifth day, she moves on the ninetieth, and is born on the ninth month; but if she that is formed on the sixtieth day, moves the hundred and tenth, and will be born on the tenth month. I treat the more largely hereof, that the reader may know, the reasonable soul is not propagated by the parents, but is infused by the Almighty, when the child hath its perfect form, and is exactly distinguished in its lineaments.

Now as the life of every other creature, as Moses shews, is in the blood; so the life of man consisteth in the soul, which although subject to passion, by reason of the gross composures of the body, in which it has a temporary confinement; yet it is immortal, and cannot in itself corrupt, or suffer change, it being a spark of the Divine Mind; and that every man has a peculiar soul, plainly appears by the vast difference between the will, judgment, opinion, manners, affections, in men. And this David observes, saying, "God hath formed the hearts and "minds of all men, and has given to every one his "own being, and a soul of its own nature." Hence Solomon rejoiced, that God had given him a happy soul, and a body agreeable to it. It has been disputed among the learned, in what part of the body the soul resides; and some are of opinion, its residence is in the middle of the heart, and from thence communicates itself to every part, which Solomon in the fourth of the Proverbs, seems to affirm, when he says, "Keep "thy heart with all diligence, for out of it are the "issues of life." But many curious physicians, searching the works of nature in man's anatomy, do affirm, that its chief seat is in the brain, from whence proceed the senses, faculties and actions, diffusing the operation of the soul through all the parts of the body, whereby it is enlivened with heat and force to the heart, by the arteries, cordites, or sleepy arteries; which part upon the throat, the which, if they happen to be broken, or cut, they cause barrenness; and if stopped, an apoplexy; for there must necessarily be ways through which the spirits, animal and vital, may have intercourse, and convey native heat from the soul. For though the soul hath its chief seat in one place, it operates in every part, exercising every member, which are the soul's instruments by which she discovers her power. But if it happen that any of the organical parts are out of tune, its whole work is confused, as appears in idiots and madmen though in some of them, the soul by a vigorous exerting its power, recovers its innate strength, and they become right after a long despondency in mind; but in others it is not recovered again in this life. For as a fire under ashes, or the sun obscured from our sight by thick clouds, afford not their full lustre, so the soul overwhelmed in moist or morbic matter is darkened, and reason thereby over-clouded, and though reason shines less in children than such as are arrived to maturity, yet no man must imagine that the soul of an infant grows up with the child, for then would it again decay; but it suits itself to nature's weakness, and the imbecility of the body wherein it is placed, that it may operate the better. And as the body is more and more capable of receiving its influence, so the soul does more and more exert its faculties, having force and endowments at the time it enters the form of a child in the womb, for its substance can receive nothing less. And thus much to prove the soul comes not from the parents, but is infused by God: I shall next prove its immortality, and so demonstrate the certainty of our resurrection.

That the soul of man is a divine ray, infused by the Sovereign Creator, I have already proved, and now come to shew that whatever immediately proceeds from him, and participates of his nature, must be as immortal as its original; for though all other creatures are endowed with life and motion, yet they want a reasonable soul, and from thence it is concluded, that their life is in their blood and that being corruptible, they perish and are no more; but man being endowed with a reasonable soul, and stamped with the Divine Image, is of a different nature, and though his body be corruptible, yet his soul being of an immortal nature cannot perish, but must, at the dissolution of his body, return to God who gave it, either to receive reward or punishment. Now that the body can sin of itself is impossible; because wanting the soul, which is the principal of life, it cannot act, nor proceed to any thing either good or evil: for could it do so, it might sin even in the grave, but it is plain that after death there is a cessation; for as death leaves us so judgment will find us.

Now reason having evidently demonstrated the soul's immortality, the holy scriptures do abundantly give testimony to the truth of the resurrection as the reader may see by perusing the fourteenth and ninth chapters of Job, and the fifth of St. John. I shall therefore leave the further discoursing of this matter to divines, whose proper province it is, and return to treat of the works of nature.

CHAP. V.

Of Monsters, and monstrous Births, and the several Reasons thereof, according to the Opinion of the Ancients; also whether Monsters are endowed with reasonable Souls, and whether Devils can engender, is briefly here discussed.

BY the ancients monsters are ascribed to depraved conceptions, and are designed to be excursions of nature, which are vicious one of these four ways, either in figure, magnitude, situation or number.

In figure, when a man bears the character of a beast, as did the beast in Saxony.

In magnitude, when one part doth not equalize with another. As when one part is too big or too little for the other parts of the body; and this is so common among us I need not produce a testimony for it.

I proceed to the cause of their generation, which is either divine or natural: The divine cause proceeds from God's permissive will, suffering parents to bring forth abominations for their filthy and corrupt affections, which are let loose into wickedness like brute beasts that have no understanding; wherefore it was enacted among the ancient Romans, that those which were any ways deformed, should not be admitted into religious houses. And St. Jerome was grieved in his time, to see the deformed and lame offered up to God in religious houses. And Keckerman, by way of inference, excludeth all that are ill-shaped, from this presbyterian function in the church. And that which is of more force than all, God himself commanded Moses not to receive such to offer sacrifices among his people, and he renders the reason, Lev. xxi. 28. "Lest he pollute my sanctuaries." Because the outward deformity of the body, is often a sign of the pollutions

30 *Aristotle's Master-Piece completed.*

of the heart, as a curse laid upon the child for the parents incontinency: Yet it is not always so, let us therefore duly examine, and search out the natural cause of their generation, which (according to the ancients, who have dived into the secrets of nature) is either in the matter, or in the agent, in the seed, or in the womb.

The matter being the default two ways, by defect or by excess: By defect when the child hath but one arm, by excess when it hath three hands or two heads.

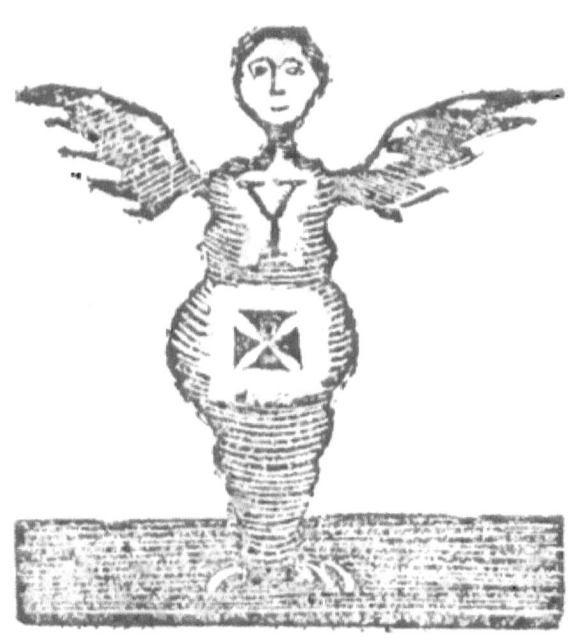

There was a monster born at Ravenna, in Italy, in the year 1512, of this kind.

Some monsters are begot by women's unnatural lying with beasts; as in the year 1630 there was a monster begotten by a woman's generating with a dog, which monster from its naval upwards had the perfect resemblance of its mother, but from its navel downwards it resembled a dog, as you may see here:

The agent or womb may be in fault three ways: 1st. In the formative faculty which may be too strong or too weak, by which is procured a depraved figure. 2dly, In the instrument or place of conception, the evil conformation or disposition where-

(See Page 35.)

32 *Aristotle's Master-Piece completed.*

Another monster representing an hairy child. It was all covered with hair like a beast. That which rendered it more frightful was, that his navel was in the place where his nose should stand, and his eyes placed where his mouth should have been, and his mouth was in the chin. It was of the male kind, and was born in France in the year 1597, at a town called Arles in Provence, and lived a few days, affrighting all that beheld it. It was looked upon as a fore-runner of those dissolations which soon after happened in that kingdom, where men, towards each other, were more like beasts than human creatures.

Where children thus are born with hairy coats,
Heaven's wrath unto the kingdom it denotes.

Of this kind was the monster born at Nazara in the year 1530, it had four arms and four legs as you see here.

LIKEWISE,

In the time of Henry III. there was a woman delivered of a child having two heads and four arms, and the body was joined to the backside. The heads were so placed, they looked contrariwise, each had two distinct arms and hands; they would both laugh, both speak, and both cry, and be hungry together, sometimes the one would speak, and the other would keep silence, and sometimes both speak together. It lived several years, but one outlived the other three years, carrying the dead one, (for there was no parting then) till the other fainted with the burden, and more with the stink of the dead carcase.

AND ALSO,
By the following figure you may see that though some of the members may be wanting, yet they are supplied by other members.

Ariſtotle's Maſter-Piece completed. 35

(This follows from Page 31.)

will cauſe a monſtrous birth. 3dly. In the imaginative power, at the time of conception, which is of ſuch a force, it ſtamps the character of the thing imagined upon the child. So that the children of an adultreſs may be like her own huſband though got by another man, which is cauſed through the force of imagination which the woman hath of her own huſband in the act of coition; and I have heard of a woman, who, at the time of conception, beholding the picture of a blackamore, conceived and bro't forth an Ethiopian. I will not trouble you with more human teſtimonies, but conclude with a ſtrong warrant. We read, Gen. xxx. 31. how Jacob having agreed with Laban, to have all the ſpotted sheep for keeping his flock, to augment his wages, took hazel rods and peeled white streaks in them, and laid them before the sheep when they came to drink, and coupled together there, whilst they beheld the rods, conceived and brought forth spotted young.

The imagination also works on the child after conception, for which I have a pregnant instance—a worthy gentlewoman in Suffolk, who being with child, and passing by her butcher killing her meat, a drop of blood sprang on her face, whereupon she said her child would have a blemish on the face, and at the birth it was found marked with a red spot.

And it is certain that monstrous births often happen by means of undue copulation, for some there are who have been long absent from one another, and have an eager desire of enjoyment, consider not as they ought to do what their circumstances are; and if it happen that they come together when the woman's menses are flowing, will notwithstanding proceed to the act of copulation, which is both unclean and unnatural; and the issue of such copulation does often prove monstrous, as a just punishment of lying together when nature forbids; and therefore though men should be ever so eager for it, yet women, knowing their own conditions, should at such times refuse their company. And though such copulations do not always produce monstrous births, yet the children then begotten are generally heavy, dull and sluggish, and defective in their understandings, wanting the vivacity and liveliness which children got in proper seasons are blessed withal.

It remains that I now make some enquiry, whether those that are born monsters have reasonable souls, and are capable of resurrection. And here both divines and physicians are generally of opinion, that those, who according to the order of generation, deduced from our first parents, proceed by natural means from either sex, though their outward shape may be deformed and monstrous, having notwithstanding a reasonable soul, and consequently their bodies are capable of a resurrection, as other mens and womens are. But those monsters that are not begotten by men, but are the product of woman's unnatural lust, in copulating with other creatures, shall perish as the brute beasts by whom they were begotten, not having a reasonable soul, or any breath of the Almighty infused into it.

And such can never be capable of a resurrection. And the same is also true in imperfect and abortive births.

Some are of opinion, that monsters may be ingendered by some infernal spirit. Of this mind was Agidus Facius, speaking of a deformed monster, born at Cracovia, and Hironemus Gardanus wrote of a maid that was got with child of a devil, she thinking it had been a fair young man; the like also is recorded by Vicentius of the prophet Merlin, that he was begot by an evil spirit.

But what a repugnance would it be both to religion and nature if the devils could beget men; when we are taught to believe, that not any was ever begotten without human seed except the Son of God. —The devil then being a spirit, having no corporeal substance, has therefore no seed of generation: To say that he can use the act of generation effectually, is to affirm that he can make something of nothing, and consequently to affirm the devil to be God, for creation belongs to God only.

Again—If the devil could assume to himself a dead body and enliven the faculties of it, and make it able to generate, as some affirm he can, yet his body must bear the image of the devil; and it borders upon blasphemy to think that God should so far give leave to the devil, as out of God's image to raise his own diabolical offspring. In the school of nature we are taught the contrary, viz. that like begets like; therefore of a devil man cannot be born, yet it is not denied, but the devils transforming themselves into human shapes, may abuse both men and women, and with wicked people use carnal copulation; but that any such unnatural conjunction can bring a human creature, is contrary both to nature and religion.

CHAP. VI.

A Discourse of the happy State of Matrimony, as it is appointed of God, and the true Felicity that redounds thereby to either Sex, and to what end it is Ordained.

WITHOUT doubt, the uniting of hearts in holy wedlock is of all conditions the happiest, for then a man has a second self, to whom he can unravel his thoughts, as well as a sweet companion in his labor; he has one in whose breast as in a safe cabinet, he may repose his inmost secrets, especially where reciprocal love and inviolate faith is settled; for there no care, fear, jealousy, mistrust, or hatred can ever interpose. For what man ever hated his own flesh, and truly a wife, if rightly considered, as our grandfather observed, is or ought to be esteemed of every honest man, bone of his bone, and flesh of his flesh, &c. Nor was it the least care of the Almighty to ordain so near an union, and that for two causes, the first for increase of posterity, the second to bridle and bind man's wandering desires and affections: nay, that they might be yet happier when God had joined them together, he blessed them, as it is in the ii. of Genesis. Columila contemplating this happy state, tells out of the

Economy of Xenophon, that the marriage bed is not only the most pleasant, but profitable course of life, that may be entered on for the preservation and increase of posterity; wherefore since marriage is the most safe, sure, and delightful station of mankind, who is exceeding prone, by the dictates of nature, to propagate his like, he does in no ways provide amiss for his own tranquillity who enters into it, especially when he comes to maturity of years, for there are many abuses in marriage, contrary to what is ordained, which in the ensuing chapter I shall expose to view.

But to proceed, seeing our blessed Saviour and his holy apostles detested unlawful lust, and pronounced those to be excluded the kingdom of heaven, that polluted themselves with adultery and whoring, I cannot conceive what face persons can have to colour their impieties, who, hating matrimony, make it their study how they may live licentiously; but in so doing, they rather seek to themselves torment, anxiety and disquietudes, than certain pleasure, besides the hazard of their immortal soul; for certain it is, mercenary love, (or as the wise man calls them) harlots smiles, cannot be true and sincere, and therefore not pleasant, but rather a net laid to betray such as trust in them into all mischief, as Solomon observes, by the young men void of understanding, who turned aside to the harlot's house. As a bird to the snare of the fowler, or an ox to the slaughter, till the dart be struck through the liver. Nor in this case can they have children, those endearing pledges of conjugal affection; or if they have, they will rather redound to their shame than comfort, bearing the odious brand of bastards: Harlots, likewise, are like swallows flying in the summer season of prosperity, but the black stormy weather of adversity coming, they take wings and fly into other regions; that is, seek themselves other lovers, but a virtuous chaste wife, fixing her entire love upon her husband, and submitting to him as her head and king, by whose directions she ought to steer in all lawful courses, will, like a faithful companion, share patiently with him in all adversities, run with cheerfulness through all difficulties and dangers, though ever so hazardous, to preserve or assist him in poverty, sickness, or whatever other misfortunes may befall him; acting according to her duty in all things; but a proud, imperious harlot will do more than she lists in the sun-shine of prosperity; and, like a horse-leech, ever craving and never satisfied, still seeming displeased if all her extravagant cravings be not answered, not regarding the ruin and misery she brings upon him by these means, though she seems to doat upon him, using to confirm her hypocrisy with crocodile's tears, vows and swoonings, when her cully is to depart awhile, or seems but to deny her immoderate desires; yet this lasts no longer than she can gratify her appetite and prey upon his fortune. Remarkable is the story that Cornardus Gosmer tells us of a young man travelling from Athens to Thebes, who met by the way a beautiful lady, as to his appearance she seemed adorned with all perfections of beauty, glittering with gold and precious stones. This seeming fair one saluted him, and inviting him to her house, not far off, pretending to be exceedingly enamoured with him, and declared she had a long time waited for an opportunity to find him alone, that she might reveal her passion to him. The young spark went with her, and when he came to her house, he found it, to appearance, built very stately, and very well furnished; which so far wrought upon his covetous inclination, that he resolved to put off his intended journey, and yield to her enticements; but whilst she was leading him to see the pleasant places adjoining to the house, came up a holy pilgrim, who seeing in what danger the youth was, resolved to set him in his right senses, and shew him what he imagined real, was quite otherwise; so that by powerful prayer the mist was taken from before his eyes, who then beheld his lady ugly, deformed and monstrous, and that whatever had appeared glorious and beautiful, was only trash. Then he made her confess what she was, and her design upon the young man, which she did, saying, she was one of the Lamiæ or Fairies, and that she had thus enchanted him on purpose to get him into her power, that she might devour him. This passage may be fully alluded to harlots, who draw those that follow their misguiding lights into the place of danger, till they have caused them to shipwreck their fortunes, and then leave them to struggle with the storms of adversity which they have raised. Now on the contrary, a loving, chaste, and even-tempered wife, seeks what she may to prevent such dangers, and in every condition does all to make him easy. And, in a word, as there is no content in the embraces of a harlot, so there is no greater joy than in the reciprocal affection and endearing embraces of a loving, obedient and chaste wife. Nor is that the principal end for which matrimony was ordained, but that the man might follow the law of his creation, by the increasing of his kind, and replenish the earth, for this was the injunction laid upon him in Paradise before his fall.—To conclude, a virtuous wife is a crown and ornament to her husband, and her price is above rubies, but the ways of a harlot are deceitful.

CHAP. VII.
Of errors in Marriage, why they are, and the Prejudice of them.

BY errors in marriage, I mean the unfitness of the persons marrying to enter into this state, and that both with respect to age and the constitution of their bodies; and therefore those that design to enter into that condition ought to observe their ability, and not run themselves upon inconveniencies; for those that marry too young, may be said to marry unseasonably, not considering their inability, nor examining the force of nature; for some, before they are ripe for consummation of so weighty a matter, who either rashly of their own accord, or by the instigation of procurers of marriage-brokers, or else forced thereto by their parents, who covet a large dowry, take upon them this yoke to their prejudice, by which some, before the expiration of a year, have been so enfeebled, that all their vital moisture has been exhausted, which hath not been restored again without great trouble and the use of medicines.— Wherefore my advice is, that it is no ways convenient to suffer children, or such as are not of age, to marry or get children; but he that proposes to marry, must observe to choose a wife of an honest stock, descended of temperate parents, being chaste, well bred, of good manners. For, if a woman have good conditions, she hath portion enough. That of Alcmenia in Plautus, is much to the purpose, where he brings in a young woman speaking.

I take not that to be my dowry, which
 The vulgar sort do wealth and honor call,
But all my wishes terminates in this,
 T' obey my husband and be chaste withal;
To have God's fear and beauty on my mind,
 To do those good who're virtuously inclin'd.

And I think she was in the right of it, for such a wife is more precious than rubies.

It is certainly the duty of parents to be careful in bringing up their children in the ways of virtue, and to have regard to their honor and reputation, and especially of virgins, when grown to be marriageable. For as has been before noted, if through the too much severity of parents, they may be crossed in their love, many of them throw themselves into the unchaste arms of the next alluring tempter that comes in the way, being, through the softness and flexibility of their nature, and the strong desire they have after what nature strongly incites them to, easily induced to believe man's false vows of promised marriage to cover their shame, and then too late their parents repent of their severity, which has brought an indeliable stain upon their families.

Another error in marriage is, the inequality of years in the parties married; such as for a young man, who, to advance his fortune, marries a woman old enough to be his grandmother, between whom, for the most part, strife, jealousies, and discontents are all the blessings which crown the genial bed, it being impossible for such to have any children.— The like may be said, though with a little excuse, when an old doting fellow marries a virgin in the prime of her youth and vigor, who, while he vainly strives to please her, is thereby wedded to his grave. For as in green youth it is unfit and unseasonable to think of marriage, so to marry in old age is altogether the same; for they that enter upon it too soon are soon exhausted, and fall into consumptions and divers other diseases, and those that procrastinate and marry unseemly fall into the like inconveniencies; on the other side, having only this honor, of an old man they become young cuckolds, especially if their wives have not been trained up in the paths of virtue, and lie too much open to the importunity and temptation of lewd and debauched men. And thus much for the errors of rash, inconsiderate and inconsiderable marriages.

CHAP. VIII.

The Opinion of the Learned concerning Children, conceived and born within Seven months, with arguments upon the Subject, to prevent suspicion of Incontinency, and bitter contests on that account. To which are added, Rules to know the disposition of Man's Body by the Genital parts.

MANY bitter quarrels happen between men and their wives, upon the man's supposition that his child came too soon, and by consequence that he cou'd not be the father; whereas it was thro' want of understanding the secrets of nature, that brought the men into that error; and which had he known, might have cured him of his suspicion and jealousy; to remove which, I shall endeavor to prove that it is possible, and has been frequently known, that children have been born at seven months. The cases of this nature that have happened, have made work for the lawyers, who have left it to the physicians to judge, by viewing the child, whether it be a child in seven, eight, or ten months.——Paul, the counsellor, has this passage, in the nineteenth book of pleading, viz. It is now a received truth, that a perfect child may be born in the seventh month, by the authority of the learned Hypocrates, and therefore we must believe that a child born at the end of the seventh month in lawful matrimony, may be lawfully begotten. Galen is of opinion, that there is no certain time set for bearing of children; and that from Pliny's authority, who makes mention of a woman that went thirteen months with child, but as to what concerns the seventh month, a learned author said—I know several married people in Holland that had twins born in the seventh month, who lived to old age, having lusty bodies, and lively minds. Wherefore their opinion is absurd, who assert, that a child at seven months cannot be perfect and long lived; and that he cannot in all parts be perfect till the ninth month, thereupon this author proceeds to tell a passage from his own knowledge, viz. Of late, says he, there happened a great disturbance among us, which ended not without bloodshed, and was occasioned by a virgin, whose chastity had been violated, descended of a noble family, of unspotted fame. Now several charged the fact upon the judge, who was president of a city in Flanders, who stifly denied it, saying, he was ready to take his oath that he never had any carnal copulation with her, and that he would not father that which was none of his. And farther argued, that he verily believed that it was a child born in seven months, himself being many miles distant from the mother of it, when it was conceived, whereupon the judges decreed, that the child should be viewed by able physicians, and experienced women, and that they should make their report; who having made diligent enquiry, all of them with one mind, concluded the child (without respecting who was the father) was born within the space of seven months, and that it was carried in the mother's womb but twenty-seven weeks and odd days; but if she should have gone full nine months, the child's parts and limbs would have been more firm and strong, and the structure of the body more compact, for the skin was very loose, and the breast-bone that defends the heart, and the gristle that lay over the stomach lay higher than naturally they should be; not plain, but crooked and sharp ridged, or pointed like those of a young chicken, hatched in the beginning of spring. And being a female infant, it wanted nails upon the joints of the fingers, upon which, from the musculous, or cartilaginous matter of the skin, nails that are very smooth to come, and by degrees harden, she had instead of nails a thin skin or film. As for her toes, there was no sign of nails upon them, wanting the heat which was expanded to the fingers, from the nearness of the heart. All this being considered, and above all, one gentlewoman of quality that assisted, affirming that she had been the mother of nineteen children, and that divers of them had been born and lived at seven months; they, without favor to any party, made their report, that the infant was a child of seven months, though within the seventh month, for in such cases, the revolution of the moon ought to be observed, which perfects itself in four bare weeks, or somewhat less than twenty-eight days, in which space of the revolution, the blood being agitated by the force of the moon, ought the courses of the woman to flow from them, which being spent, and the matrix being cleansed from the menstruous blood, which happens on the fourth day, then if a man on the seventh day lie with his wife, the copulation is most natural, and then is the conception best, and the child thus begotten may be born in the seventh month, and prove very healthful: So that upon this report the supposed father was pronounced innocent, upon proof that he was one hundred miles distant all that month in which the child was begotten; and as for the mother, she strongly denied that she knew the father, being forced in the dark, and so through fear and surprize was left in ignorance.

As for coition it ought not to be had unless the parties be in health, least it turn to the disadvantage of the children so begotten, creating in them, thro' the abundance of ill humours, divers languishing diseases, wherefore health is no way better to be discerned than by the genitals of the man. For which reason midwives, and other skilful women, were formerly wont to see the testicles of children, thereby to conjecture their temperature and state of body; and young men may know thereby the signs or symptoms of death; for if the cases of the testicles be loose and feeble, and the cods fall down, it denotes that the vital spirits, which are the props of life, are fallen; but if the secret parts be wrinkled and raised up, it is a sign all is well; but that the event may exactly answer the prediction, it is necessary to consider what part of the body the disease possesseth; for if it chance to be the upper part that is afflicted, as the head or stomach, then it will not so well appear by the members, which are unconcerned with such grievances; but the lower part of the body exactly sympathizing with them, their liveliness on the contrary makes it apparent; for nature's force, and the spirits that have their intercourse, first manifest themselves therein, which occasion midwives to feel the genitals of children, to know in what part the grief is resided, and whether life or death be portended thereby, the symptoms being strongly communicated by the vessels, that have their intercourse with the principal seat of life.

CHAP. IX.

Of the Green Sickness in Virgins, with its Causes, Signs, and Cures; together with the chief occasion of Barrenness of Women, and the means to remove the Cause, and render them Fruitful.

THE Green Sickness is so common a distemper in virgins, especially those of a phlegmatic complexion, that it is easily discerned, shewing itself by discolouring the face, making it look green, pale, and of a dusty colour; proceeding from raw and indigested humours; nor doth it only appear to the eye, but sensibly affects the person with difficulties of breathings, pains in the head, palpitations of the heart, with unusual breathings, and small throbbings of the arteries in the temples, neck, and back, which often casts them into fevers, when the humour is over vicious; also loathing of meat, and the distention of the hypocondrian part, by reason of the inordinate affluction of the menstruous blood to the greater vessels; and from the abundance of humours the whole body is often troubled with swelling, or at least the thighs, legs, and ancles, all above the heels. There is also a great weariness of the body without any reason for it.

The Galenical physicians affirm that this distemper proceeds from the womb, occasioned by the abundance of gross, vicious, and rude humours arising from several inward causes; but there are also outward causes, which have a share in the production of it; as taking cold in the feet, drinking of water, intemperance of diet, eating of things contrary to nature, viz. Raw or burnt flesh, ashes, coals, old shoes, chalk, wax, nut-shells, mortar, lime, oatmeal, tobacco pipes, &c. Which occasion both a suppression of the menses, and obstructions through the whole body; therefore the first thing necessary to vindicate the cause is matrimonial conjunction, and such copulation as may prove satisfactory to her that is afflicted; for then the menses will begin to flow, according to their natural and due course, and the humours being dispersed will soon waste themselves; and then no more matter being admitted to increase them, they will vanish, and a good temperament of body will return; but in case this best remedy cannot be had soon enough, then blood her in the ancles; and if she be about the age of sixteen, you may likewise do it in the arm, but let her blood but sparingly, especially if the blood be good. If the disease be of any continuance, then it is to be eradicated by purging, preparation of the humour first considered, which may be done by the virgin's drinking of decoct of guiacum, with dittany of Creete; but the best purge in this case, ought to be made of aloes, agric, senna, rhubarb; and for strengthening the bowels, and opening obstructions, chalybeat medicines are chiefly to be used. The diet must be moderate, and sharp things by all means avoided.—And for finding the humours, take prepared steel, bezoar stone, the root of scotzonera, oil of chrystal in small wine, and let the diet be moderate, but in no wise let vinegar be used therewith, nor upon any occasion. And in so observing, the humours will be dilated and dispersed, whereby the complexion will return, and the body be lively and full of vigor.

And now since barrenness daily creates discontent, and that discontent breeds difference between man and wife, or by immediate grief frequently casts the woman into one or other distemper, I shall in the next place treat thereof.

Of Barrenness.

Formerly before women came to the marriage-bed, they were first searched by the midwife, and those only which she allowed of as fruitful were admitted. I hope therefore it will not be amiss to shew you how they may prove themselves, and turn the barren ground into a fruitful soil. Barrenness is a deprivation of life and power, which ought to be in seed, to procreate and propogate. For which end men and women were made.

Causes of barrenness. It is caused by over-much cold or heat, driving up the seed, and corrupting it, which extinguishes the life of the seed, making it waterish and unfit for generation. It may be caused also by not flowing, or overflowing of the courses, by swellings, ulcers, and inflammations of the womb, by an excrescence of flesh growing about the matrix, by the mouth of the womb being turned to the back or side, by fatness of the body, whereby the mouth of the matrix is closed up, being pressed with the omentum, or caul, and the matter of the seed is turned too fat; or if she be of a lean and dry body to the world, she proves barren; because though she doth conceive, yet the fruit of her body will wither before it comes to perfection, for want of nourishment. Silvius ascribes one cause of barrenness to compelled copulation; as when parents force their daughters to have husbands contrary to their liking, therein marrying their bodies not their hearts, and where there is a want of love, there, for the most part is no conception; as very often appears in women which are deflowered against their wills. Another main cause of this barrenness, is attributed to want of a convenient moderating quality which the woman ought to have with the man; as if he be hot, she must be cold; if he be dry, she must be moist; but but if they be both dry, or both moist of constitution they cannot propagate; and yet simply considered of themselves, they are not barren; for he and she who were before as the barren fig tree, being joined to an apt constitution, become as the fruitful vine. And that a man and woman being every way of like constitution cannot procreate, I will bring nature itself for a testimony, who hath made man of the better constitution than woman, that the quality of the one may moderate the quality of the other.

Signs of Barrenness.

If barrenness doth proceed from over-much heat, she is of a dry body, subject to anger, hath black hair, quick pulse, her purgations flow but little, and that with pain, she loves to play in the courts of Venus. But if it comes by cold, then are the signs contrary to those even now recited. If through the evil quality of the womb, make a suffumigation of red storax, myrrh, cassia wood, nutmeg, cinnamon; and let her receive the fume of it into the womb, covering her very close; and if the odour so received, passeth through the body up into the mouth and nostrils, of herself she is fruitful; but if she feels not the fume in her mouth and nose, it argues barrenness one of these ways, that the spirit of the seed is either through cold extinguished, or through heat dissipated. If any woman be suspected to be unfruitful, cast natural brimstone, such as are digged out of the mine, in her urine; and if worms breed therein, of herself she is not barren.

Prognostics. Barrenness makes women look young, because they are free from those pains and sorrows which other women are accustomed to bring forth withal. Yet they have not the full perfection of health which fruitful women do enjoy, because they are not rightly purged of the menstruous blood, and superfluous seed, which two, are the principal cause of most uterine diseases.

Cure. First the cause must be removed, and the womb strengthened, and the spirits of the seed enlivened.

If the womb be over hot; take syrup of succory with rhubarb. syrup of violets, endive, roses, cassia, purslain. Take of endive, water-lilies, borage-flowers, of each a handful; rhubarb, mirobalan of each three drams, with water make a decoction, and to the straining of the syrup, electuary of violets one ounce, syrup of cassia half an ounce. manna three drams; make a potion: Take of syrup of mugwort one ounce, syrup of maiden-hair two ounces; pul'y, elect, triasand one dram, make a julep. Take pru. falut. elect. rof. mesuæ of each three drams, rhubarb one scruple, and make a bolus, apply to the reins and privities fomentations of the juice of letice, violets, roses, mallows, vine leaves, and night shade;

anoint the secret parts with the cooling unguent of Galen.

If the power of the seed be extinguished by cold, take every morning two spoonfuls of cinnamon water, with one scruple of mithridate: Take syrup of calamint, mugwort, betony, of each one ounce; waters of penny-royal, feverfew, hyssop, sage, of each two ounces, make a julep: Take oil of anniseed two scruples and an half; diacimini, diachiathi, diamosci, diaglaànga of each one ounce, sugar four ounces, with water of cinnamon, make lozenges, take of them a dram and half twice a day, two hours before meals; fasten cupping-glasses to the hips and belly. Take of styrax, calamint, one ounce, mastick, cinnamon, nutmeg, lign, aloes, frankincense, of each half an ounce, musk ten grains, ambergrease, half a scruple, with rose water, make a confection, divide it into four equal parts, of one part make a pomum odoratum to smell on, if she be not hysterical; of the second make a mass of pills, and let her take three every night; of the third make a pessary, dip it in the oil of spikenard and put it up; of the fourth make a suffumigation for the womb.

If the faculties of the womb be weakened, and the life of the seed suffocated by over much humidity flowing to these parts. Take of betony, marjoram, mugwort, penny-royal, balm, of each a handful, roots of alloin, fennel, of each two drams, anniseed, cummin, of each one dram, with sugar and water a sufficient quantity, make a syrup, and take three ounces every morning.

If barrenness proceeds from dryness, consuming the matter of the seed; take every day almond milk, and goats milk extracted with honey. But often of the root satyron candied, and of the electuary of diasyren. Take three wedders heads, boil them until all the flesh come from the bones, then take melilot, violets, camomile, mercury, orchis with their roots, of each a handful, fennigreek, lintseed, valerian roots, of each one pound, let all these be decocted in the aforesaid broth, and let the woman sit in the decoction up to the navel.

If barrenness be caused by any proper effect of the womb, the cure is set down in the second part; sometimes the womb proves barren when there is no impediment on either side, except only in the manner of the act; as when in the emission of the seed, the man is quick and the woman too slow, whereby there is not an emission of both seeds at the same instant as the rules of conception requires; before the acts of coition foment the private parts with the decoction of betony, sage hyssop, and calimint; and anoint the mouth and neck of the womb with musk and civet

The cause of barreness being removed, let the womb be corroborated as follows:

Take of bay berries, mastick, nutmeg, frankincense, nuts, laudanum, galbanum, of each one dram, styracis liquid two scruples, cloves half a scruple, ambergrease two grains, then with oil of spikenard make a pessary.

The aptest time for conception is instantly after the menses are ceased, because then the womb is thirsty and dry, apt both to draw the seed, and return it, by the roughness of the inward superficies. And besides, in some the mouth of the womb is turned into the back or side, and is not placed right until the last day of the courses.

Excess in all things is to be avoided; lay aside all passion of the mind, shun study and care, as things that are enemies to conception; for if a woman conceives under such circumstances, how wise soever the parents are, the children at the best will be but foolish, because the animal faculties of the parent, viz. the understanding and the rest (from whence the child derives its reason) are, as it were confused, through the multiplicy of cares and cogitations; examples hereof we have in learned men, who after great study and care, instantly accompany with their wives, often beget very foolish children. A hot and moist air is most convenient, as appears by the women in Egypt, who usually bring forth three or four children at one time.

CHAP. X.

Virginity, what it is, in what it consists, and how violated; together with the Opinion of the Learned about the Mutation of the Sex in the Womb, during the operation of Nature in framing the Body.

THERE are many ignorant people that boast of their skill in the knowledge of virginity, and some virgins have undergone hard censures through their ignorant determinations; and therefore I tho't it highly necessary to clear this point, that the towering imaginations of conceited ignorance may be brought down, and the fair sex (whose virtues are so illustriously bright, that they both excite our wonder, and command our imitation) may be freed from the calumnies and detractions of ignorance and envy; and so their honors may continue as unspotted, as they have kept their persons uncontaminated, and free from defilement.

Virginity in a strict sense does signify the prime, the chief, the best of any thing, which make men so desirous of marrying virgins, imagining some secret pleasure to be enjoyed in their embraces, more than in those of widows, or such as before hath been lain withal; though not many years ago, a very great person was of another mind, and to use his own expressions " that the getting of a maiden-head was " such a piece of drudgery, as was more proper for "a porter than a prince." But this was only his opinion, for moſt men I am ſure, have other ſentiments. But to our purpoſe,

The curious inquirers into nature's ſecrets have obſerved, that in young maids in the ſinu pudoris, or in that place which is called the neck of the womb, is that pondous production, vulgarly called the hymen, but more rightly the clauſtrum virginale, and in the French, "button de roſe," or roſe bud, becauſe it reſembles the bud of a roſe expanded, of a conve gilly flower. From hence is derived the word defloro, or deflower. And hence taking away virginity is called deflowering a virgin. Moſt being of opinion, that the virginity is altogether loſt when this duplication is fractured and diſſipated by violence; and when it is found perfect and entire, no penetration has been made; and it is the opinion of ſome learned phyſicians that there is not either hymen or ſkin expanded, containing blood in it, which divers think in the firſt copulation flows from the fractured expanſe.

Now this clauſtrum or virginale, or flower, is compoſed of four carbuncles or little buds like myrtleberries, which in virgins are full and plump, but in women flag and hang looſe; and theſe are placed in the four angles of the ſinus pudoris joined together by little membranes and ligatures like fibres, each of them ſituated in the teſticles, or ſpaces between each carbuncle, with which in a manner they are proportionably diſtended, which membranes being once delacerated, denote devirgination; and many inquiſitive, and yet ignorant perſons finding their wives defective herein the firſt night of their marriage, have thereupon ſuſpected their chaſtity, concluded another had been there before them. Now to undeceive ſuch, I do affirm, that ſuch fractures happen divers accidental ways, as well as by copulation with men, viz. by violent ſtraining, coughing, sneezing, stopping of urine, and violent motion of the vessels, forcibly sending down the humors, which pressing for passage, break the ligatures or membrane; so that the intireness of fracture of that which is commonly taken for their virginity or maiden-head, is no absolute sign of dishonesty; though certain it is, that it is more frequently broke in copulation than by any other means.

I have heard, that at an assize held at Rutland a young man was tried for a rape, in forcing a virgin; when after divers questions asked, and the maid swearing positively to the matter, naming the time, place, and manner of the action; it was upon mature deliberation resolved, that she should be searched by a skilful surgeon and two midwives, who were to make their report upon their oaths: which after due examination, they accordingly did, affirming, that the membranes were entire, and not delacerated; and that it was their opinion, for that reason, that her body had not been penetrated. Which so far wrought with the jury, that the prisoner was acquitted; and the maid afterwards confessed, she swore against him out of revenge, he having promised to marry her, and afterwards declined it. And this much shall suffice to be spoken concerning virginity.

I shall now proceed to something of nature's operation, in mutation of sexes in the womb.

This point is of much necessity, by reason of the different opinions of men relating to it; therefore before any thing positively can be asserted, it will be altogether convenient to recite what has been delivered, as well in the negative as affirmative. And first, Severus Pinæus who argues for the negative, writes thus: The genital parts of both sexes are so unlike others in substance, composition, situation, figure, action and use, that nothing is more unlike; and by how much more all parts of the body (the breasts excepted which in women swell more, because nature ordained them for suckling the infant,) have exact resemblance; so much more do the genital parts of the one sex compared with the other differ; and if their figure be thus different, much more in their use. The venerial appetite also proceeds from different causes; for in man it proceeds from a desire of emission, and in woman from a desire of reception, in women also, the chief of those parts are concave, and apt to receive, but in men they are more porous.

These things considered, I cannot but wonder (added he) how any one can imagine, that the genital members of the female births should be changed unto those that belong to males, since by those parts only the distinction of sexes is made; nor can I well impute the reason of this vulgar error to any thing, but the mistake of unexpert midwives, who have been deceived by the evil conformation of the parts, which in some male births may have happened to have some small protrusions, not to have been discerned; as appears by the example of a child christened at Paris by the name of Joan as a girl, which afterwards proved a boy; and on the contrary, the over far extension of the clytoris in female births may have occasioned the like mistakes. Thus far Pliny proceeds in the negative: And yet notwithstanding what he has said, there are divers learned physicians that have asserted the affirmative of which number Galen is one. A man (saith he) is different from a woman in nothing else but having his genital members without the body; but a woman hath them within. It is certain, that if nature having formed, should convert him into a woman, she hath no other task to perform, but to turn his genital members inward; and so turn a woman into a man by the contrary operation; but this is to be under-

D

stood of the child when it is in the womb, and not perfectly formed; for divers times nature hath made a female, and it hath so remained in the womb of the mother for near a month or two, and afterward plenty of heat increasing in the genital members, they have issued forth, and the child has become a male, yet retaining some certain gestures unbefitting the masculine sex; as female actions, a shrill voice, and a more effeminate temper than ordinary: contrariwise, nature having often made a male, and cold humours flowing to it, the genitals being inverted, yet still retaining a masculine air both in voice and gestures. Now, though both these opinions are supported by several reasons, yet I esteem the latter more agreeable to truth, for there is not that vast difference between the genitals of the two sexes, as Pliny would have us believe there is, for a woman has in a manner the same members with the man, though they appear not outward, but are inverted for the conveniency of generation: the chief difference being that the one is solid, and the other porous, and the principal reason for changing sexes is, and must be attributed to heat or cold, suddenly and slowly contracted, which operates according to its greater or lesser force.

CHAP. XI.

Directions and Cautions for Midwives, and how first a Midwife ought to be qualified.

A MIDWIFE that would acquit herself well in her employment, ought by no means to enter upon it rashly or unadvisedly, but with great caution, considering that she is accountable for all the mischief that befals through her wilful ignorance or neglect; therefore let none take upon them the of fice barely upon pretence of maturity of years, and child-bearing, for in such for the most part there are divers things wanting that ought to be observed; which is the occasion so many women and children are lost. Now, for a midwife in relation to her person, these things ought to be observed; viz. She must neither be too young nor too old, neither extraordinary fat, nor weakened by leanness, but in a good habit of body; nor subject to diseases, fears, nor sudden frights; her body well shaped, and neat in her attire; her hands smooth and small, her nails ever paired short, not suffering any rings to be upon her finger during the time she is doing her office, nor any thing upon her wrists that may obstruct. And to these ought to be added activity, and a convenient strength, with much cautiousness and diligence, not subject to drowsiness, nor apt to be impatient.

As for her manners, she ought to be courteous, affable, sober, chaste, and not subject to passion, bountiful and compassionate to the poor, and not covetous when she attends upon the rich.

Her temper chearful and pleasant, that she may the better comfort her patient in the dolorous labors; nor must she at any time make too much haste, though her business should require her in another case, lest she thereby endanger the mother of the child.

Of spirit, she ought to be wary, prudent, and cunning; but above all, the fear of God ought to have the ascendant in her soul, which will give her both knowledge and discretion, as the wise man tells us.

CHAP. XII.

Further Directions for Midwives, teaching them what they ought to do, and what to avoid.

SINCE the office of a Midwife has so great an influence on the well or ill-doing of women and children, in the first place let her be advantageous to her practice, never thinking herself so perfect, but that she may add to her knowledge by study and experience; yet never let her make an experiment at her patient's cost, nor apply any experiment in that case, unless she has tried them, or knows they will do no harm; practising neither upon poor nor rich, but speaking freely what she knows; and by no means prescribing such medicines as will cause abortion, though desired; which is a high degree of wickedness, and may be termed murder. If she be sent for to them she knows not, let her be very cautious ere she goes, lest by laying an infectious woman she endanger the spoiling of others, as sometimes it happens; neither must she make her house a receptacle for great bellied women to discharge their burdens in; lest her house get an ill name, and she thereby loose her practice.

In laying of women, if the birth happen to be large and difficult, she must not seem to be concerned but must cheer up the woman, and do what she can to make her labor easy. For which she may find directions in the second part of this book.

She must never think of any thing but doing well, causing all things to be in readiness that are proper for the work, and the strengthening of the woman, and receiving the child; and above all, let her take care to keep the woman from being unruly when her throws are coming upon her, lest she thereby endanger her own life and the child's.

She must also take care she be not too hasty in

her business, but wait God's leisure for the birth; and by no means let her suffer herself to be disordered by fear, though things should not go well, lest it should make her incapable of giving that assistance which the laboring woman stands in need of; for when we are most at a loss, then there is most need of prudence to set things right.

And now, because she can never be a skilful midwife, that knows nothing but what is to be seen outwardly; I shall not think it amiss, but on the contrary highly necessary with modesty to describe the generative parts of women, as they have been anatomized by the learned, and shew the use of such vessels as contribute to generation.

CHAP. XIII.

Of the Genitals of Women, external and internal to the Vessels of the Womb.

IF it were not for public benefit, especially of the practitioners and professors of the art of midwifery; I would forbear to treat of the secrets nature, because they may be turned by some lascivious and lewd persons into ridicule: But they being absolutely necessary to be known, in order to public good, I will not omit them, because some may make a wrong use of them. These parts that offer themselves to view at the bottom of the belly, are the fissura magna, or the great chink, with its labia or lips, the mons veneris, and the hair; these are called by the general name pudenda, from shame-facedness, because when they are bare, they begin pudor or shame upon a woman. The fissura magna reaches from the lower part of the os pubis, to within an inch of the anus, but it is lesser and closer in maids than in those that have born children; and has two lips, which towards the pubis grow thicker and more full; and meeting upon the middle of the os pubis, makes that rising hill that is called mons veneris, or the hill of **Venus**.

The next thing that offers, are the nympha and clytoris, the former of which is of a membrany and flammy substance, spungy, soft, and partly fleshy and of a red colour, in the shape of wings, two in number, though from their rise they are placed in an acute angle, producing there a fleshy substance, which clothe the clytoris; and sometimes they spread so far, that incision is required to make way for the man's instrument of generation.

The clytoris is a substance in the upper part of the division where the two wings concur, and is the seat of venereal pleasure, being like a yard in situation, substance, composition and erection; growing sometimes out of the body two inches, but that never happen unless through extreme lust, or extraordinary accidents. This clytoris consists of two pungy and skinny bodies, containing a distinct original from the os pubus, the head of it being covered with a tender skin, having a hole or passage like the penis or yard of a man; tho' not quite through, in which, and the bigness, it only differs from it.

The next thing are fleshy knobs, and the great neck of the womb; and these knobs are behind the wings, being four in number, and resemble myrtle berries, being placed quadrangular, one against the other; and in this place inserted to the orifice of the bladder, which opens itself into the fissures, to evacuate the urine; for securing of which from the cold, or the like inconveniency, one of these knobs is placed before it, and shuts up the passage.

The lips of the womb that next appear, being separated, disclose the neck thereof, and in the two things are to be observed, which is the neck itself, and the hymen, but more properly the clauſtrum virginale, of which before I have difcourfed. By the neck of the womb is to be underſtood the channel that is between the aforeſaid knobs and the inner bone of the womb, which receives the penis like a ſheath; and that it may the better be dilated for the pleaſure of procreation, the ſubſtance of it is ſinewy, and a little ſpongy; and in this concavity are divers folds, or obicular plaits made up tunicles, wrinkled like an expanded roſe. In virgins they plainly appear, but in women that have often uſed copulation they are extinguiſhed: ſo that the inner ſide of the womb's neck appears ſmooth and in old women it appears more hard and griſled. But though this channel be at ſometimes wreathed and crooked, ſinking down; yet in the time of copulation, labor, or the monthly purgation, it is erected and extended, which over extenſions occaſion the pains of child birth.

The hymen, or clauſtrum virginale, is that which cloſes the neck of the womb, being, as I have fore-cited in the chapter relating to virginity, broken in firſt copulation, its uſe being rather to ſtay the untimely courſes in virgins, than to any other end; and commonly, when broken in copulation, or by any other accident, a ſmall quantity of blood flows from it, attended with ſome little pain. From whence ſome obſerve, that between the duplicity of the two tunicles, which conſtitute the neck of the womb, there are many veins and arteries running along and ariſing from the veſſels on both ſides of the thigh, and ſo paſſing into the neck of the womb, being very large, and the reaſon thereof is, for that the neck of the bladder requires to be filled with abundance of ſpirits, thereby to be dilated for its better taking hold of the penis, there being great heat required in ſuch motions, which become more intent by the act of frication, and conſumes a conſiderable quantity of moisture, in the supply of which large vessels are altogether necessary.

Another cause of the longness of these vessels is, by reason the menses make their way through them, which often occasions women with child to continue their purgation, for though the womb be shut up, yet the passage in the neck of the womb through which the vessels pass, are open: In this case there is further to be observed, that as soon as you penetrate the pudendum, there appear two little pits or holes wherein is contained an humour, which being expunged in time of copulation, greatly delights the woman.

CHAP. XIV.

A Description of the Womb's fabrick, the preparing Vessels, and Testicles in Women; as also of the difference and ejaculatory Vessels.

IN the lower part of the hypogastrium, where the lids are widest and broadest, they being greater and broader thereabout than those of men, for which reason they have likewise broader buttocks than men, the womb is joined to its neck, and is placed between the bladder and strait gut, which keeps it from swaying or rowling, yet gives it liberty to stretch and dilate itself again to contract, nature in that case disposing it. Its figure is in a manner round, and not unlike a gourd, lessening a little and growing more acute towards one end, being knit together by its proper ligaments; its neck likewise is joined by its own substance and certain membranes that fasten unto the os sacrum, and the share bone. As to its largeness, that much differs in women, especially the difference is great between such as have borne children, and those that have borne none. In substance it is so thick that it exceeds a thimble breadth, which, after copulation is so far from decreasing, that it augments to a greater proportion, and the more to strengthen it, it is interwoven with fibres overthawrt, which are both strait and winding, and its proper vessels are veins, arteries and nerves, and among these there are two little veins which pass from the spermatick vessels to the bottom of the womb, and two larger from the hypostratic, which touch both the bottom of the neck, the mouth of these veins, piercing as far as the inward concavity.

The womb hath two arteries on both sides the spermatick vessels and the hypostratic, which will accompany the veins; and besides there are divers little nerves, that are knit and twined in the form of a net, which are also extended throughout, even from the bottom of the pudenda, themselves being placed chiefly for sense and pleasure, moving in sympathy between the head and the womb.

Now it is to be further noted, that by reason of the two ligaments that hang on either side the womb from the share bone, piercing through the peritoneum, and joined to the bone itself, the womb is moveable upon sundry occasions, often falling low or rising high. As for the neck of the womb, it is of an exquisite feeling, so that if it be at any time out of order, being troubled at any time with a schirrosity, over fatness, moisture, or relaxation, the womb is subjected thereby to barrenness; in those that are with child there frequently stays a glutinous matter in the entrance to facilitate the birth; for at the time of delivery, the mouth of the womb is opened to such a wideness as is conformable to the bigness of the child, suffering an equal dilation from the bottom to the top.

As for the preparatory or spermatick vessels in women, they consist of two veins and two arteries not differing from those of men, but only of their largeness and manner of insertion, for the number of veins and arteries is the same as in men, the right vein issuing from the trunk of the hollow vein descending, and on the side of them are two arteries, which grow from the aorta.

As to the length and breadth of these vessels they are narrower and shorter in women than in men; only observe, they are more wreathed and comforted than in men, as shrinking together by reason of their shortness, that they may by their looseness, be better stretched out when occasion requires it; and those vessels in women are carried with an indirect course through the lesser guts, the testicles, but are in midway divided into two branches, the greater goes to the stones, constituting a various or winding body, and wonderfully inosculating, the lesser branch ending in the womb, in the inside of which it disperseth itself, and especially at the higher part of the bottom of the womb for its nourishment, and that part of the courses may purge through the vessels; and seeing the testicles of women are seated near the womb, for that cause these vessels fall not from the peritonœum, neither make they much passage as in men, nor extending themselves in the share bone.

The stones in women commonly called testicles, perform not the same action as in men, they are also different in their location, bigness, temperature, substance, form and covering. As for the place of their seat, it is in the hollowness of the abdomen; neither are they pendulous, but rest upon the muscles of the loins, so that they may, by contracting the greater heat, be more fruitful, their office being to contain the ova, or eggs, one of which being impregnated by the man's seed engenders man, yet they differ from those of men in figure, by reason of their lessness or flatness at each end, not being so round or oval. The external superfices being likewise more unequal, appearing like the composition of a great many knobs and kernels mixt together. There is a difference also in their substance, they being much more soft and pliable, loose and not so well compacted.

Their bigness and temperament being likewise different, for they are much colder and lesser than those in men. As for their covering or inclosure, it differs extremely; for as mens are wrapped in divers tunicles, by reason they are extremely pendulous, and subject to divers injuries, unless so fenced by nature; so womens stones being internal, and less subject to casualty, are covered with one tunicle or membrane, which though it closely cleave to them, yet they are likewise half covered with the peritonœum.

The ejaculatory vessels are too obscure passages, one on each side, nothing differing from the spermatick veins in substance: They do rise on one part from the bottom of the womb, not reaching from the other extremity, either to the stones, or to any other part, but shut up and unpassable, adhering to the womb as the colon does to the blind gut, and winding half way about; though the testicles are remote to them, and touch them not, yet they are tied to them by certain membranes, resembling the wing of a bat, through which certain veins and arteries passing through the end of the testicles, may be turned here to have their passages proceeding from the corner of the womb to the testicles, and are accounted proper ligaments, by which the testicles and womb are united, and strongly knit together; and these ligaments in women are the cremasters in men; of which I shall speak more largely, when I come to describe the masculine parts conducing to generation.

CHAP. XV.

A Description of the Use and Action of several parts in Women appointed in Generation.

THE externals, commonly called the pudenda, are designed to cover the great orifice, and that are to receive the penis or yard, in the act of coition, and give passage to the birth and urine. The use of the wings and knobs like myrtle berries, are for the security of the internal parts, shutting the orifice and neck of the bladder, and by their swelling up, cause titulation and delight in those parts, and also to obstruct the involuntary passage of the urine.

The action of the clytoris in women is like that of a penis in man, viz. the erection, and its outer end is like the glans of the penis, and has the same name. And as the glans of man is the seat of the greatest pleasure in conception, so is this in women.

The action and use of the neck of the womb is equal with that of the penis, viz. erection, occasioned divers ways, first, in copulation it is erected and made strait for the passage of the penis in the womb —secondly, whilst the passage is repleted with spirit and vital blood, it becomes more strait for embracing the penis; and as for the conveniency of erection, it is two-fold—First, Because if the neck of the womb was not erected, the yard could have no convenient passage to the womb: Secondly, it hinders any hurt or damage that might ensue through the violent concussion of the yard, during the time of copulation.

As for the veins that pass through the neck of the womb, their voice is to replenish it with blood and spirit, that still as the moisture consumes by the heat contracted in copulation, it may, by these vessels, be renewed; but their chief business is to convey nutriment to the womb.

The womb has many properties attributed to it. As first, rentention of the fœcundated egg, and this is properly called conception. Secondly, to cherish and nourish it till nature has framed the child, and brought it to perfection. and then it strongly operates in sending forth the birth, when the time of its remaining there is expired, dilating itself in a wonderful manner, and so aptly removed from the senses, that nothing of injury can proceed from thence; retaining to itself a power and strength to operate and cast forth the birth, unless by accident it be rendered deficient; and then to strengthen and enable it, remedies must be applied by skilful hands, directions for the applying of which shall be given in the second part.

The use of the preparing vessel is this, the arteries convey the blood of the testicles; part whereof is put in the nourishment of them, and the production of those little bladders (in all things resembling eggs,) through which the vasa preparentia run, and are obliterated in them; and as for the veins, their office is to bring back what blood remains from the use aforesaid.

The vessels of this kind are much shorter in women than in men, by reason of their nearness to the stones, which defects is yet made good by the many intricate windings to which those vessels are subject; for in the middle way they divide themselves into two branches, though different in magnitude, for one being greater than the other passes to the stones.

The stones in women are very useful, for where they are defective, generation-work is at an end; for although these bladders which are on their outward superfices contain nothing of seed, as the followers of Galen and Hippocrates did erroneously imagine, yet they contain several eggs, generally

E

twenty (in each testicle) one of which being impregnated by the spirituous part of the man's seed in the act of coition, descends through the oviducts in the womb, and from hence in process of time becomes a living child.

CHAP. XVI.
Of the Organs of Generation of Man.

HAVING given you a description of the organs of generation in women, with the anatomy of the fabric of the womb; I shall now (to complete the first part of this treatise) describe the organs of generation in man, and how they are fitted to the use for which nature designed them.

The instrument of generation in man (commonly called the yard; and in Latin, penis a pendendo because it hangs without the belly,) is an organical part, which consists of skin, tendons, veins, arteries, sinews and great ligaments; and is long and round, and on the upper side flattish, seated under the ossa pubis, and ordained by nature, partly by evacuation of urine, and partly for conveying the seed into the matrix; for which end it is full of small pores, through which the seed passes into it, through the vesicula seminalis, and also the neck of the vesicula urinalis, which pours out the urine when they make water; besides the common parts, as caticula, the skin, and the membrana carnosa, it hath these proper or internal parts, viz. The two nervous bodies, the septum the urethera, the glans, four muscles, and the vessels. The nervous bodies (so called) are surrounded with a thick white previous membrane, but their inmost substance is spungy, consisting chiefly of veins, arteries, and nervous fibres interwoven together like a net; and when the nerves are filled with animal spirits, and the arteries with hot and spirituous blood, then the penis is distended and becomes erect; but when the influx of dead spirits ceases, then the blood and remaining spirits are absorbed by the veins and so the penis spirits limber and grow flaggy; below these nervous bodies is the uthera, and whenever the nervous bodies swell, it swells also. The muscles of the penis are four, two shorter arising from the coxendix, and serving its erection, and for that reason are called erectores; two larger proceeding from the spincter of the anus, and serve to dilate the uretra ejaculation of seed; and are called dilatantes, or winding. At the end of the penis is the glans, covered with a very thin membrane; by means of which and its nervous substance, it becomes most exquisitely sensible, and is the principal seat of pleasure in copulation. The utmost covering of the glans is called prœputium a perputando from being cut off, it being that which the Jews cut off in circumcision, and it is tied by the lower parts of it to the glans of the fœtus. The penis is also stocked with veins, arteries, and nerves.

The testiculi, or stones (so called) because testifying one to be a man; elaborate the blood brought to them by the spermatic arteries into seed. They have coats of two sorts, proper and common; the common are two, and invest both the testes. The outermost of the common coats consists of the caticula, or true skin; and is called the scortum, hanging out of the abdomen like a purse, the innermost is the membrana carnosa; the proper coats are also two, the outer called eliotrodes or virginales; the inner albugidia, into the outer is inserted the cremaster: the upper part of the testes is fixed; epidimydes, or pastata, from whence arise the vassa differentia or ejaculatoria which when they come near the neck of the bladder, deposite the seed into the veficule feminiales, thefe veficule feminiales are two, each like a bunch of grapes, and emit the feed into the urethera, in the act of copulation.

Near them are the proftratæ, about the bignefs of a walnut, and join to the neck of the bladder. Authors cannot agree about the ufe of them; but moft are of opinion, that they afford an oily, floppy, and fat humour to befmear the urethera, whereby to defend the fame from the acrimony of the feed and urine. But the veffels which convey the blood to the teftes out of which the feed is made, arartriæ fpermaticæ, and are alfo two. The veins which carry out the remaining blood are two, and have the name of venæ fpermaticæ.

CHAP. XVII.

A Word of Advice to both Sexes: Being feveral Directions refpecting Copulation.

SINCE nature has implanted in every creature a mutual defire of copulation, for the encreafe and propagation of its kind; and more efpecially in man, the lord of the creation, and mafter-piece of nature; that fo noble a piece of divine workmanfhip might not perifh, fomething ought to be faid concerning that, it being the foundation of all that we have hitherto been treating of; fince without copulation there can be no generation. Seeing therefore it depends fo much upon it, I thought it neceffary, before I conclude the firft part, to give fuch directions to both fexes, for the performing of that act, as may appear efficacious to the end for which nature defigned it. But it will be done with that caution, as not to offend the chafteft ear, nor put the fair fex to the trouble of a blufh in reading it. Firft, Therefore, when a married couple, from a defired of having children, are about to make use of those means that nature ordained to that purpose, it would be very proper to cherish the body with generous restoratives, so that it may be brisk and vigorous: and if their imaginations were charmed with sweet and melodious airs, and cares and thoughts of business drowned in a glass of racy wine, that their spirits may be raised to the highest pitch of ardor and joy, it would not be amiss. For any thing of sadness, trouble and sorrow, are enemies to delights of Venus: And if at such times of coition, there should be conception, it would have a malevolent effect upon children. But though generous restoratives may be used for invigorating nature, yet all excess is carefully to be avoided, for it will allay the briskness of the spirits, and render them dull and languid, and also hinders digestion, and so must needs be an enemy to copulation. For if food moderately taken that is well digested, creates good spirits, and enables a man with vigor and activity to perform the dictates of nature. It is also highly necessary, that in their natural embraces, they meet each other with an equal ardor. For if the spirits flag on either part, they will fall short of what nature requires; and the woman either miss of conception, or else the children prove weak in their bodies, or defective in their understanding; and therefore I do advise them before they begin their conjugal embraces, to invigorate their mutual desires, and make their flames burn with a fierce ardor, by those endearing ways, that love can better teach, than I can write.

When they have done what nature requires, a man must have a care he does not part too soon from the embraces of his wife, lest some sudden interposing cold should strike into the womb, and occasion a miscarriage, and thereby deprive them of the fruit of their labor.

And when after some small convenient time the man hath withdrawn himself, let the woman gently betake herself to rest with all imaginable serenity and composure of mind, from all anxious and disturbing thoughts, or any other kind of perturbation: And let her, as much as she can, forbear turning herself from that side on which she first reposed; and by all means let her avoid coughing or sneezing, which by its violent concussion of the body, is a great enemy to conception, if it happen soon after the act of coition.

The End of the First Book.

A PRIVATE LOOKING-GLASS
FOR THE
FEMALE SEX.

PART SECOND.

TREATING OF SEVERAL MALADIES INCIDENT TO THE WOMB, WITH PROPER REMEDIES FOR THE CURE OF EACH.

CHAP. I.
Of the Womb in general.

ALTHOUGH in the First Part I have spoken something of the fabric of the womb, yet being in the Second Part to treat more particularly thereof, and of the various distempers and maladies it is subject to; I shall not think it tautology, to give you, by way of instruction, a general description both of its situation and parts, but rather think this Second Part would be imperfect without it, for that it can by no means be omitted, especially since in it I am to speak of the menstruous blood.

First—Touching the Womb: Of the Grecians it is called Metra, the mother; Adelphos saith Priscian, because it makes us all brothers.

It is placed in hypogastrium, or lower part of the body, in the cavity called pelvis, having the strait gut on one side, to keep it from the other side of the back bone, and the bladder on the other side to defend it from blows. The form or figure of it is like a virile member, only thus excepted; the manhood is outward, and womanhood within.

It is divided into the neck and the body:—The neck consists of a hard fleshy substance, much like a cartilage, at the end thereof there is a membrane traversly placed, called hymen, or engion; near unto the neck there is a prominant pinnacle, which is called, of Montanus, the door of the womb, because it preserveth the matrix from cold and dust. Of the Grecians it is called clytoris, of the Latins perputium muliebre, because the Jewish women did abuse those parts to their own mutual lusts, as St. Paul speaks, Rom. i. 26.

The body of the womb is that wherein the child is conceived. And this is not altogether round, but dilates itself into two angles; the outward part of it is nervous and full of sinews, which are the cause of its motion, but inwardly it is fleshy. It is fabulously reported, that in the cavity of the womb there are seven divided cells, or receptacles for human seed. But those that have seen anatomies, do know there are but two; and likewise, that these two are not divided by a partition, but only by a line, or future running through the midst of it. In the right side of the cavity, by reason of the left side, by the coldness of the spleen, females are begotten.

And this do most of our moderns hold for an infallible truth, yet Hippocrates holds it but in the general: For in whom, saith he, the spermatic vessels on the right side come from the reins, and the spermatic vessels on the left side from the hollow vein, in them males are conceived in the left side, and females in the right. Well, therefore, may I conclude with the saying of Epidocles—Such sometimes is the power of the seed, that a male may be conceived in the left side, as well as in the right. In the bottom of the cavity there are little holes called the cotilendons, which are the end of certain veins and arteries, serving in breeding women to convey substance to the child, which is received by the umbilical veins; and others to carry the courses into the matrix.

Now touching the menstruels—they are defined to be a monthly flux of excrementitious and unprofitable blood.

In which we are to note, that the matter flowing forth is excrementitious; which is to be understood of the superplus or redundance of it; for it is an excrement in quality, its quantity being pure and incorrupt, like unto the blood in the veins.

And that the menstruous blood is pure and subtile of itself, all in one quality with that in the veins, is proved two ways: First, From the final cause of the blood, which is the propagation and conservation of mankind; that man might be conceived, and being begotten, he might be comforted and preserved both in the womb and out of the womb. And all will grant it for a truth, that a child while it is in the matrix, is nourished with the blood; and it is true, that being out of the womb it is still nourished with the same, for the milk is nothing but the menstruous blood made white in the breast; and I am sure woman's milk is not thought to be venomous, but of a nutritive quality, answerable to the tender nature of the infant. Secondly—It is proved to be true from the generation of it, it being the superfluity of the last aliment of the fleshly parts.

It may be objected—If the body be not of a hurtful quality, how can it cause such venomous effects? As if the same fall upon trees and herbs, it maketh the one barren, and mortifieth the other. Averves writes: That if a man accompany with any menstruous woman, if she conceive she shall bring forth a leper. I answer—This malignity is contracted in the womb; for that wanting native heat to digest this superfluity, sends it to the matrix, where seating itself until the mouth of the womb be dilated, it becomes corrupt and venomous, which may easily be, considering the heat and moisture of the place. This blood therefore being out of its vessels, it offends in quality. In this sense let us understand Pliny, Cornelius Florus, and the rest of that torrent. But if frigidity be the cause why women cannot digest all their last nourishments, and consequently that they have these purgations, it remains to give a reason why they are of so cold a constitution more than a man, which is this.

The natural end of man and woman's being is to propagate; and this injunction was imposed upon them by God at their first creation, and again after the deluge. Now in the act of conception there must be an agent and patient, for if they be both every way of one constitution, they cannot propagate; man therefore is hot and dry, woman cold and moist; he is the agent, she the patient, or weaker vessel, that she should be subject to the office of the man. It is necessary the woman should be of a cold constitution, because in her is required a redundancy of nature for the infant depending on her; for otherwise, if there were not a superplus of nourishment for the child, more than is convenient for the mother, then would the infant detract and weaken the principal parts of the mother, and like unto the viper, the generation of the infant would be the destruction of the parent.

The monthly purgations continue from the fifteenth year to the forty-sixth or fiftieth. Yet often there happens a suppression, which is either natural or morbifical, they are naturally suppreft in breeding women, and such as suck. The morbifical suppression falls now into our method to be spoken of.

CHAP. II.
Of the Retention of the Courses.

THE suppression of the terms is an interception of that customary evacuation of blood, which, every month, should come from the matrix, proceed from the instrument or matter vitiated, the part affected is the womb, and that of itself or by consent.

CAUSE.] The cause of this suppression is either external or internal. The external cause may be heat or dryness of the air, immoderate watching, great labor, vehement motion, &c. whereby the matter is so confused, and the body so exhausted, that there is not a superplus remaining to be expelled, as is recorded of the Amazons, who, being active, and always in motion, had their fluxations very little, or not at all. Or it may be caused by cold, which is most frequent, making the blood vicious and gross, condensing and binding up the passages that it cannot flow forth.

The internal cause is either instrumental or material, in the womb or in the blood.

In the womb it may be divers ways; by a posthumes, humors, ulcers, by the narrowness of the veins and passages, or by the omentum or kell in fat bodies, pressing the neck of the matrix; but then they must have hernia zirthilis; for in mankind the kell reacheth not so low. By over much cold or heat, the one vitiating the action, and the other consuming the matter by an evil composition of the uterine parts, by the neck of the womb being turned aside, and sometimes, though rarely, by a membrane or excrescence of the flesh growing about the mouth or neck of the womb. The blood may be in fault two ways, in quantity or quality. In quantity, when it is so consumed, that there is not a superplus left, as in virgoes, or virile women, who, tho' their heat and strength of nature, digest and consume all in their last nourishment.

SIGNS.] Signs manifesting the disease, are pains in the head, neck, back and loins, weariness of the whole body, but especially of the hips and legs, by reason of a confinity which the matrix hath with these parts, trembling of the heart; particular signs are these, if the suppression proceed from cold, she is heavy, sluggish, of a pale colour, and has a slow pulse; Venus's combats are neglected, the urine crudle, waterish, and much in quantity, the excrements of the guts usually are retained. If of heat, the signs are contrary to those now recited. If the retention be natural, and come of conception, this may be known by drinking of hydromel, that is water and honey after supper, going to bed, and by the effect which it worketh; for after taking it, she feels a beating pain upon the navel, and lower part of the belly, it is a sign she hath conceived, and that the suppression is natural; if not, then it is vicious, and ought medicinally to be taken away.

PROGNOSTICS.] With the evil quality of the womb the whole body stands charged, but especially the heart, the liver and the brain; and betwixt the womb and these three principal parts there is a singular concert. First, the womb communicates to the heart, by the mediation of those arteries which come from aorta. Hence the terms being suppress'd, will ensue faintings, swoonings, intermission of pulse, cessation of breath. Secondly, It communicates to the liver, by the veins derived from the hollow vein. Then will follow obstructions, cahexies, jaundice, dropsies, hardness of spleen. Thirdly, It communicates to the brain, by the nerves and membrane of the back, hence will arise epilepsis, frenzies, melancholy, passion, pain in the after parts of the head, fearfulness, inability of speaking. Well, therefore, may I conclude with Hippocrates—If the months be suppreſt, many dangerous diseases will follow.

CURE.] In the cure of this, and of all other following effects, I will observe this order. The cure muſt be taken from chirurgical pharmacutical, and diuretical means. This ſuppreſſion is a plethoric effect, and muſt be taken away by evacuation. And therefore we will firſt begin with phlebotomy. In the midſt of the menſtruel period, open the liver vein; and for the reverſion of the humour, two days before the wonted evacuation, open the saphena on both feet: if the repletion be not great, apply cupping glaſſes to the legs and thighs, altho' there be no hope to remove the ſuppreſſion.

After the humour hath been purged, proceed to make proper and forcible remedies. Take of trochiſks of myrrh, one dram and an half; parſley seed, caſtor rhinds, or caſſia, of each one ſcruple; and of the extract of mugwort one ſcruple and an half; muſk ten grains with the juice of ſmallage: make twelve pills, take ſix every morning, or after ſupper going to bed.

If the retention comes from repletion or fulneſs, let the air be hot and dry, uſe moderate exerciſe before meals, and your meat and drink attenuating; ſeethe with your meat, garden ſavory, thyme, origane, and cyche peaſon; if of emptineſs, or defect of matter, let the air be moiſt and moderate hot; ſhun exerciſe, and watchings, let your meat be nouriſhing and of a light digeſtion, as rare eggs, lamb, chickens, almonds, milk and the like.

CHAP. III.
Of the Overflowing of the Courses.

THE learned say, by comparing of contraries truth is made manifest. Having therefore spoken of the suppression of terms, order requires now that I should insist on the overflowing of them, an effect no less dangerous than the former, and this immoderate flux of the month is defined to be a sanguinous excrement proceeding from the womb, exceeding in both quantity and time: First, It is said to be sanguinous, the matter of the flux being only blood, wherein it differs from that which is commonly called the false courses or whites, of which I shall speak hereafter. Secondly, It is said to proceed from the womb, for there are two ways by which the blood flows forth, the one way is by the internal veins in the body of the womb, and this is properly called the monthly flux. The other is by those veins which are terminated in the neck of the matrix, and this is called of Etius the hemorhoids of the womb. Lastly, It is said to exceed both in quantity and time. In quantity, saith Hippocrates, when they flow about eighteen ounces; in time, when they flow above three days; but we take this for a certain character of their inordinate flowing, when the faculties of the body thereby are weakened: in bodies abounding with gross humours, this immoderate flux sometimes unburthens nature of her load, and ought not to be staid without the counsel of a physician.

CAUSE.] The cause of this affair is internal or external; the internal cause is threefold, in the matter, instrument, or faculty: The matter, which is in the blood, may be vicious two ways—First, By the heat of constitution, climate, or season heating the blood, whereby the passages are dilated, and the faculty weakened, that it cannot retain the blood Secondly, By falls, blows, violent motion, breaking of the veins, &c.

The external cause may be calidity of the air, lifting, carrying of heavy burthens, unnatural child-birth, &c.

SIGNS.] In this inordinate flux the appetite is decayed, the conception deprived, and all the actions weakened; the feet are swelled, the colour of the face is changed, and a general feebleness possesseth the whole body: If the flux comes by the breaking of a vein, the body is sometimes cold, the blood flows forth on heaps, and that suddenly, with great pains. If it comes through heat, the orifice of the vein being dilated, then is there little or no pain; yet the blood flows faster than it doth in an erosion, and not so fast as it doth in a rupture. If by erosion or sharpness of blood, she feels a great heat scalding the passage, it differs from the other two, in that it flows not so suddenly, nor so copiously as they do: If by weakness of the womb, she abhorreth the use of Venus. Lastly, If it proceed from an evil quality of the blood, drop some of it on a cloth, and when it is dry, you may judge of the quality of the colour. If it be choleric, it will be yellow; if melancholy, black; if phlegmatic, waterish and whitish.

PROGNOSTIC.] If with the flux be joined a convulsion, it is dangerous, because it intimates the more nobler parts are vitiated, and a convulsion caused by emptiness is deadly: If it continues long, it will be cured with great difficulty, for it was one of the miracles that our Saviour Christ wrought to cure this disease, when it had continued twelve years. To conclude—If the flux be inordinate, many diseases will ensue, and without remedy, the blood, together with the native heat, being confumed, either cachectical, hydropical, or pareletical diseases will follow.

CURE.] The cure consisteth in three particulars: First, In repelling and carrying away the blood.—Secondly, In correcting and taking away the fluxability of the matter. Thirdly, In corroberating the veins and faculties: For the First, to cause a repression of the blood, open a vein in the arm, and draw out so much blood, as the strength of the patient will permit; and that not together, but at several times, for thereby the spirits are less weakened, and the refraction so much the greater.

Apply cupping glasses to the breasts, and also the liver, that the reversion may be in the fountain.

To correct the fluxability of the matter, cathartical means, moderated with the astrictories may be used.

If it be caused by erosion, or sharpness of blood, consider whether the erosion be by salt phlegm, or adust choler; if by salt phlegm, prepare with syrup of violets, wormwood, roses, citron peel, succory, &c. Then take this purgation following; Mirobulana, chebel, half an ounce; trochisks of agaric, one dram, with plaintain water, make a decoction, add thereunto sir, roseat, lax, three ounces, and make a potion.

It by adust choler, prepare the body with syrup of roses, myrtles, sorrel, purslain, mix with water of plantain, knot-grass, and endive——then purge with this potion: Take rhind of mirobulana, rhubarb, of each one dram; cinnamon, fifteen grains; infuse them one night in endive water; add to the straining pulp of tamerine, cassia, of each half an ounce; syrup of roses an ounce; make a potion:—If the blood be waterish or unconcoct, as it is in the hydropical bodies, and flow forth by reason of the tenuity or thinness to draw off the water, it will be profitable to purge with agaric, elaterium, coloquirtida: Sweating is proper in this case, for thereby the matter offending is taken away, and the motion of the blood carried to the outward parts. To procure sweat, use carduus water, with mithridate, or the decoction and sarsaparilla. The gum of guaiacum also, greatly provoke sweat; pills of sarsaparilla, taken every night going to bed, are worthily commended. If the blood flows forth through the opening or breaking of a vein, without any evil quality of itself, then ought only corroboratives to be applied, which is the last thing to be done in this inordinate flux.

The air must be cold and dry; all motion of the body is forbidden; let her meat be pheasant, partridge, mountain birds, coneys, calves feet, &c.— And let her beer be mixt with the juice of pomegranates and quinces.

CHAP. IV.
Of the Weeping of the Womb.

THE weeping of the womb is a flux of blood, unnatural, coming from thence in drops, after the manner of tears, causing violent pains in the same, keeping neither period nor time. By some it is referred unto the immoderate evacuation of the course, yet they are distinguished in the quantity and manner of overflowing, in that they flow copiously and free; in this continually, though by little and little, and that with great pain and difficulty, wherefore it is likened unto the stranguary.

The cause is in the faculty, instrument, or matter. In the faculty by being enfeebled, that it cannot expel the blood, and the blood resting there, makes the part of the womb grow hard, and stretcheth the vessels from whence proceedeth the pain of the womb:

In the inſtrument by the narrowneſs of the paſſages.—Laſtly, It may be the matter of the blood, which may offend in too great a quantity, or in an evil quality. It being groſs and thick, that it cannot flow forth as it ought to do, but by drops. The ſigns will beſt appear by the relation of the patient: Hereupon will iſſue pains in the head, ſtomach, and back; with inflammations in the head, ſtomach, and back; with inflammation, ſuffocations, and excoriations of the matrix: If the ſtrength of the patient will permit, firſt open a vein in the arm, rub the upper parts, and let her arms be corded, that the force of the blood may be carried backward; then apply ſuch things as may laxate and molify the ſtrengthening the womb, and aſſuage the ſharpneſs of the blood, as cataplaſms made of brand, lintſeed, fenugreek, meliot, mallows, mercury, and artiplex: If the blood be vicious and groſs, add thereto mugwort, calamint, dictam, and betony; and let her take of Venice treacle, the quantity of a nutmeg, the ſyrup of mugwort every morning, make injections of the decoctions of mallows, mercury, lintſeed, grounſel, mugwort, fenugreek, with oil of ſweet almonds.

Sometimes it is cauſed by wind, and then phlebotomy is to be omitted, and in the ſtead thereof take ſyrup of feverfew an ounce; honey, roſes, ſyrup of roſes, ſyrup of flæchus, of each half an ounce. Water of calamint, mugwort, betony, hyſſop, of each an ounce: make a julep, if the pain continues, take this purgation. Take ſpechieræ, one dram; diacatholicon, half an ounce; ſyrup of roſes, laxatives one ounce; with the decoction of mugwort, and the four cordial flowers, make a potion. If it comes through the weakneſs of the faculty, let that be corroborated—If through the groſſneſs and ſharpneſs of the blood, let the quality of it be altered, as I have ſhewn in the foregoing chapter.——

Lastly, If the excrements of the guts be retained, provoke them by glyster of the decoctions of camomile, betony, feverfew, mallows, lintseed juniper berries, common seed, anniseed, meliote, adding thereto diacatholicon, half an ounce; salt nitre, a dram and an half. The patient must abstain from salt, sharp, and windy meat.

CHAP. V.
The false Courses or Whites.

FROM the womb proceeds not only menstruous blood, but accidently many other excrements, which, by the ancients, are comprehended under the title of robus gunakois, which is a distillation of a variety of corrupt humours through the womb, flowing from the whole body, or part of the same, keeping neither course nor colour, but varying in both.

COURSE.] The cause is either promiscuously in the whole body, by a cacochymia, or weakness of the same, or in some of the parts; as in the liver, which, by the inability of the sanguifacative faculty, causeth a generation of corrupt blood; and the matter is reddish, sometimes the gall being sluggish in its office, not drawing away those choleric superfluities ingendered in the liver; and the matter is yellowish sometimes in the spleen, not descending and cleansing the blood of the dregs of excrementious parts. And then the matter flowing forth, is blackish: It may also come from the cattarahs in the head, or from any other putrified or corrupted member: but if the matter of the flux be white, the cause is either in the stomach or reins. In the stomach by a phlegmatical and crude matter there contracted and variated, through grief, melancholy, and other distempers; for otherwise, if the matter were only petnical, crude, phlegm, and no ways corrupt, being taken into the liver, it might be converted into blood; for phlegm in the ventricle is called nourishments half digested; but being corrupt, though sent into the liver, yet it cannot be turned into nutriment; for the second decoction cannot correct that which the first hath corrupted; and therefore the liver sends it to the womb, which can neither digest, nor repel it, and so it is voided out with the same colour it hath in the ventricle. The cause also may be in the reins, being overheard, whereby the spermatical matter, by reason of its thinness, flows forth. The external causes may be moistness of the air, eating of corrupt meats, anger, grief, slothfulness, immoderate sleeping, costiveness in the body.

The signs are exturbation of the body, shortness and stinking of the breath, loathing of meat, pain in the head, swelling in the eyes and feet, melancholy; humidity flows from the womb of divers colours, as red, black, green, yellow, and white. It differs from the flowing and overflowing of the courses, in that it keeps no certain period, and is of many colours, all which do generate from blood.

Prognostics.] If the flux be phlegmatical, it will continue long, and be difficult to cure: yet if vomiting, for diarhæ happeneth, diverts the humour, it cures the disease. If it be choleric, it is not so permanent, yet more perilous, for it will cause a cliff in the neck of the womb, and sometimes make an excoriation of the matrix; in melancholic it must be dangerous contumacious; yet the flux of the hemerhoids administers cure.

If the matter flowing forth be reddish, open a vein in the arm; if not, apply litagures to the arms and shoulders: Galen glories of himself, how he cured the wife of Brutus laboring of this disease, by rubbing the upper part with crude honey.

If it is caused by a distillation from the brain take syrup of betony, stochas and marjoram, purge with pill coch, fine quibus de agarico; make nasalia of the juice of sage, hyssop, betony, nigella, with one drop of the oil of elect. dianth. aromat. rosat, diambræ, diomesch, dulcis, of each one dram; nutmeg, half a dram; with sugar and betony water, make lozenges, to be taken every morning and evening. Auri Alexandrina half a dram at night going to bed. If these things help not, use the suffumigation and plaister, as they are prescribed.

If it proceeds from crudites in the stomach, or from a cold distempered liver, take every morning of the decoction of lignum sanctum; purge with pill de agrico, de hermodact, de hiera, diacolinthid, fœtid, agrigatio; take elect. aromat, roses, two drams; citron pill dried, nutmeg, long pepper, of each one scruple, with mint water, and make lozenges of it. Take of them before meals; if the frigidity of the liver there be joined a repletion of the stomach, purging by vomit is commendable; for which take three drams of the electuary diasaru. Galen allows of diuretical means as absum, ptrosolinan.

If the matter of the flux be choleric, prepare the humour with syrup of roses, violets, endive, succory; purge with mirobolans, manna, rhubarb, cassia. Take of rhubarb two drams, anniseed one dram, cinnamon a scruple and an half; infuse them in six ounces prune broth; add too the straining of manna an ounce, and take in the morning according to art. Take spicerum, diatonlanton, diacorant, prig diarthod, abbaris, diacydomes, of each one dram, sugar four ounces, with plaintain water, make lozenges. If the clyster of the gall be sluggish, and do not stir up the faculty of the gut, give glysters, with the decoction of four molifying herbs, with honey of roses and aloes.

If the flux be melancholous, prepare with syrup of maiden-hair, epithymium, polipody, borrage buglos, fumitary, hart's tongue, and syrupus bisatius, which must be made without vinegar, otherwise it will rather animate the disease than nature; for melancholy, by the use of vinegar, is encreased, and both by Hippocrates, Sylvius, and Avenzoar, it is disallowed of as an enemy to the womb, and therefore not to be used inwardly in all uterine diseases.

Lastly—Let the womb be cleansed from the corrupt matter, and then corroborated; for the purifying thereof make injections of the decoction of betony, feverfew, spikenard bistrot, mercury, sage, adding thereto sugar, oil of sweet almonds, of each two ounces; pessaries also may be made of silk, cotton, modified in the juice of the aforementioned herbs.

CHAP. VI.

Of the Suffocation of the Mother.

THIS effect (which if simply considered) is none but the cause of an effect, is called in English the suffocation of the mother; not because the womb is strangled, but for that it causeth the womb to be choaked. It is a retraction of the womb towards the midriff and stomach, which presseth and crusheth up the same, that the instrumental cause of respiration, the midriff is suffocated; and consenting with the brain, causing the animating faculty, the efficient cause of respiration, also to be intercepted, where the body being refrigerated and the action depraved, she falls to the ground as one being dead.

In these hysterical passions some continue longer, some shorter: Rabbi Moses writes of some who lay in the paroxysy of the fit for two days. Rufus makes mention of one who continued in the same passion three days and three nights, and at the three days end she revived. That we may learn by other mens harms to beware, I will tell you an example, Parœus writeth of a woman in Spain who suddenly fell into an uterine suffocation, and appeared to mens judgment as dead; her friends wondering at this her sudden change, for their better satisfaction sent for a surgeon to have her dissected, who beginning to make an incision, the woman began to move, and with great clamour returned to herself again, to the horror and admiration of all the spectators.

That you may distinguish the living from the dead, the ancients prescribe three experiments: The first is to lay a light feather to the mouth, and by its motion you may judge whether the patient be living or dead. The second is—to place a glass of water on the breast, and if you perceive it to move, it betokeneth life. The third is—to hold a pure looking glass to the mouth and nose, and if the glass appears thick with a little dew upon it, it betokeneth life. And these three experiments are good, yet with this caution, that you ought not to depend on them too much, for though the feather and the water do not move, and the glass continue pure and clear, yet it is not a necessary consequence that she is destitute of life; for the motion of the lungs, by which the respiration is made, may be taken away that she cannot breathe, yet the internal transpiration of the heat may remain, which is not manifest by the motion of the breast or lungs, but lies occult in the heart and inward arteries; examples whereof we have in the fly and swallow, which in the cold of winter seem dead, and breathe not at all; yet they live by the transpiration of that heat which is reserved in the heart and inward arteries; therefore when the summer approacheth, the internal heat being revocated to the inward parts, they are then again revived out of their sleepy ecstacy.

Those women therefore that seem to die suddenly, and upon no evident cause, let them not be committed to the earth unto the end of three days, left the living be buried for the dead.

Cause.] The part affected in the womb, of which there are a twofold motion, natural and symptomatical. The natural motion is, when the womb attracteth the human seed, or excludeth the infant or secundine. The symptomatical motion of which we are to speak, is a convulsive drawing of the womb.

Signs.] At the approaching of the suffocation, there is a paleness of the face, weakness of the legs, shortness of breath, frigidity of the whole body, with a working up into the throat, and then she falls down at once void both of sense and motion; the mouth of the womb is closed up, and being touched with the finger feels hard, the paroxism of the fit once past, she openeth her eyes, and feeling her stomach opprest, she offers to vomit.

Prognostics.] If the disease hath its being from the corruption of the seed, it foretells more danger than if it proceeded from the suppression of the courses, because the seed is concocted and of a purer quality than the menstruous blood; and the more pure being corrupted, becomes the more foul and filthy, as appears in eggs, the purest nourishment, which vitiated, will yield the noisomest savour. If it be accompanied with a syncope, it shews nature is but weak, and that the spirits are almost exhausted; but if sneezing follows, it shews the heat that was almost extinct, doth now begin to return, and that nature will subdue the disease.

Cure.] In the cure of this effect, two things must be observed: First, That during the time of the paroxism, nature be provoked to expel those malignant vapours which bind up the senses, that she may be recalled out of the sleepy ecstasy. Secondly,

That in the intermission of the fit, proper medicines be applied to take away the cause.

To stir up nature, fasten cupping-glasses to the hips and navel, applying ligatures unto the thighs; rub the extreme parts with salt, vinegar, and mustard; cause loud clamours and thunderings in the ears. Apply to the nose assafœtida castor, and sagapaneum steeped in vinegar, provoke her to sneeze by blowing up into her nostrils the powder of castor, white pepper, pellitory of Spain, and hellebore. Hold under her nose partridge feathers, hair and old shoes burnt, and all other stinking things, for evil odours are an enemy to nature; hence the animal spirits do so contest and strive against them that the natural heat is thereby restored. The brain is so opprest sometimes, that we are compelled to burn the outward skin of the head with hot oil, or with a hot iron. Sharp clysters and suppositories are available. Take of sage, calamint, harehound, feverfew, marjoram, betony, hyssop, of each one handful; annifeed half an ounce; coloquotinda, white hellebore, sal. gem. of each two drams; boil these in two pounds of water to the half; add to the straining oil of castor two ounces; hiera picra two drams, and make a glyster of it.

If it be caused by the retention and corruption of the seed, at the instant of the paroxism, let the midwife take oil of lillies, marjoram and bays, dissolving in the same two grains of civet; add as much musk; let her dip her finger therein, and put into the neck of the womb, tickling and rubbing the same.

The fit being over, proceed to the curing of the cause. If from the retention of the seed, a good husband will administer a cure, but those who cannot honestly purchase that cure, must use such things as will dry up and diminish the seed; as diciminua, diacalaminthes, &c. Amongst batonics, the seed of angus castus is well esteemed of, whether taken inwardly, applied outwardly, or receive a suffumigation. It was held in great honor amongst the Athenians, for by it they did remain as pure vessels and preserved their chastity by only strowing it on the bed whereon they lay, and hence the name of angus castus given it, as denoting its effects. Make an issue in the inside of each leg, an hand breadth below the knee. Make trochisks of agric two scruples, wild carrot-seed, lign aloes, of each half a scruple; washed turpentine, three drams, with conserve of anthos make a bolus; castor is of excellent use in this case, eight drams of it taken in white wine, or you may make pills of it with mithridite, and take them going to bed. Take of white briony root dried, and after the manner of carrots, one ounce; put into a draught of wine, placing it by the fire, and when it is warm drink it; take myrrh, castor, asofœtida, of each one scruple; saffron and rue seed, of each four grains; make eight pills, and take two every night going to bed.

Galen, by his own example, commends unto us agaric pulverized, of which he frequently gave one scruple in white wine; lay to the navel at bed time a head of garlic bruised, fastening it with a swithing-band; make a girdle of galbacum for the waist, and also a plaister for the belly, placing in one part of it civet and musk, which must be laid upon the navel. Take pulveris benedict, trochisk of agaric, of each two drams; mithridite a sufficient quantity, and so make two pessaries, and it will purge the matrix of wind and phlegm, foment the natural part with salad oil, in which has been boiled rue, feverfew and camomile.

CHAP. VII.
Of descending or falling of the Mother.

THE falling down of the womb is relaxation of the ligatures, whereby the matrix is carried backward, and in some hangs out in the bigness of an egg. Of these there are two kinds, distinguished by a descending and precipitation. The descending of the womb is, when it sinks down to the entrance of the privities, and appears to the eye either not at all, or very little. The precipitation is, when the womb, like a purse, is turned inside outward, and hangs betwixt the thighs in the bigness of a cupping-glass.

Cause.] The cause is external or internal: The external cause is difficult child-birth, violent pulling away the secundine, rashness and inexperience in drawing away the child, violent coughing, sneezing, falls, blows, and carrying heavy burthens.— The internal cause, in general, is overmuch humidity flowing into these parts, hindering the operation of the womb, whereby the ligaments by which the womb is supported is relaxed.

The cause, in particular, is referred to be in the retention of the seed, or in the suppression of the monthly courses.

Signs.] The arse, gut and bladder oftentimes are so crushed that the passage of both excrements are hindred; if the urine flows forth white and thick, and the midriff is molested, the loins are grieved, the privities pained, and the womb sinks down to the private parts, or else comes clean out.

Prognostics.] This grief possessing an old woman is cured with great difficulty, because it weakens the faculty of the womb, and therefore though it be reduced into its proper place, yet upon very little illness or indisposition it is subject to return; and so it also is with the younger sort, if the disease be inveterate. If it be caused by a putrefaction in the nerves it is incurable.

Cure.] The womb being naturally placed between the strait gut and the bladder, and now fallen down, ought to be put up again, until the faculty both of the gut and bladder be stirred up; nature being unloaded of her burden, let the woman be laid on her back in such sort, that her legs may be higher than her head; let her feet be drawn up to her hinder parts, with her knees spread abroad; then mollify the swelling with oil of lillies and sweet almonds, or with the decoction of mallows, beets, fenugrek, and lintseed: When the inflammation is dissipated, let the midwife anoint her hand with oil of mastick, and reduce the wound into its place.

CHAP. VIII.

Of the Inflammation of the Womb.

THE phlegmon, or inflammation of the matrix, is an humour possessing the whole womb, accompanied with unnatural heat, by obstruction and gathering together of corrupt blood.

Cause.] The cause of this effect is suppression of the menses, repletion of the whole body, immoderate use of Venus, often handling the genitals, difficult child-birth, vehement agitation of the body, falls, blows; to which also may be added the use of sharp pessaries, whereby not seldom the womb is inflamed, cupping-glasses also fastened to the pubis and hypogastrium, draw the humours to the womb.

Signs.] The signs are anguish, humours, pain in the head and stomach, vomiting, coldness of the knees, convulsions of the neck, doating, trembling of the heart; often there is a straitness of breath, by reason of the heat which is communicated to the midriff, the breasts sympathizing with the womb, pained and swelled. Further, if the forepart of the matrix be inflamed, the privities are grieved, the urine is suppreft, or flows forth with difficulty. If the after-part, the loins and back suffer, the excrements are retained; if the right side, the right hip suffers, the right leg is heavy, slow to motion, in so much, that sometimes she seems to halt. And so if the left side of the womb be inflamed, the left hip is pained, and the left leg is weaker than the right.— If the neck of the womb be refreshed, the midwife putting up her finger shall feel the mouth of it retracted, and closed up with hardness about it.

Prognostics.] All inflammations of the womb are dangerous, if not deadly; and especially if the total substance of the matrix be inflamed; yet they are perilous if in the neck of the womb. A flux of the belly foretells health, if it be natural, for nature works best by the use of her own instruments.

Cure.] In the cure, first let humours flowing to the womb be repelled; for effecting of which, after the belly has been loosened by cooling clysters, phlebotomy will be needful; open therefore a vein in the arm (and if she be not with child) the day after strike saphenna on both feet, fasten ligatures and cupping-glasses to the arm, and rub the upper part. Purge lightly with cassia, rhubarb, senna, morobolans. Take of senna two drams; anniseed one scruple; mirobolans half an ounce; barley water a sufficient quantity; make a decoction, dissolve in it syrup of succory, with rhubarb two ounces; pulp of cassia half an ounce; oil of anniseed two drops, and make a potion.

The air must be cold, all motion of the body, especially of the lower parts, is forbidden, vigilance is commended; for by sleep the humours are carried inward, by which the inflammation is increased; eat sparingly, let your drink be barley water, clarified whey, and your meat chickens and chicken-broth, boiled with endive, succory, sorrel, bugloss and mallows.

CHAP. IX.

Of the Schirrosity or Hardness of the Womb.

OF phlegmon neglected, or not perfectly, is generated a schirrus of the matrix; which is a hard unnatural swelling, insensibly hindering the operations of the womb, and disposing the whole body to slothfulness.

Cause.] One of this disease may be ascribed to want of judgment in the physician, as many empirics, administering to an inflammation of the womb, do overmuch refrigerate and astringe the humour, that it can neither pass forward nor backward, hence the matter being condensed, degenerates into a lapidious hard substance. Other causes may be suppression of the menstruous retention of the lochia, commonly called the after purgings, eating of corrupt meats, as in the disordinate longing called pica, to which breeding women are so often subject. It may proceed also from obstructions and ulcers in the matrix, or from evil effects of the liver and spleen.

Signs.] If the bottom of the womb be affected, she feels as it were a heavy burthen representing a mole, yet differing in that the breasts are attenuated and the whole body waxeth less. If the neck of the womb be affected, no outward humours will appear; the mouth of it is retracted, and being touched with the finger feels hard, nor can she have the company of a man without great pains and prickings.

Prognostics.] A schirrus confirmed is incurable, and will turn into a cancer or incurable dropsy, and ending in a cancer proves deadly, because the native heat in those parts being almost smothered, can hardly again be restored.

Cure.] Where there is a repletion, phlebotomy is advisible, wherefore opening the medina on both arms, and the saphena on both feet, more especially if the menses be suppressed.

The air must be temperate; gross, vicious and salt meats are forbidden, as pork, bull's beef, fish, old cheese, &c.

CHAP. X.

Of the Dropsy of the Womb.

THE uterine dropsy is an unnatural swelling, elevated by the gathering together of wind or phlegm in the cavity, membranes or substance of the womb, by reason of the debility of the native heat and aliment received, and so it turns into an excrement.

The causes are overmuch cold or moistness of the melt and liver, immoderate drinking, eating of crude meats; all which causing a repletion, do suffocate the natural heat. It may be caused likewise by the overflowing of the courses, or by any other immoderate evacuation. To these may be added abortives, phlegmons and schirrosities of the womb.

Signs.] The signs of this effect are those, the lower parts of the belly, with the genitals, are puffed up and pained, the feet swell, the natural colour of the face decays, the appetite is depraved, and the heaviness of the whole body concurs. If she turns herself in the bed, from one side to the other, a noise like the overflowing of water is heard. Water sometimes comes from the matrix. If the swelling be caused by wind, the belly being hot, it sounds like a drum; the guts rumble, and the wind breaks thro' the neck of the womb with a murmuring noise; this effect may be distinguished from a true conception many ways, as will appear by the chapter of conception.

Prognostics.] This effect foretells the sad ruin of the natural functions, by that singular consent the womb hath with the liver; that therefore the chacevy, or general dropsy will follow.

Cure.] In the cure of this disease, imitate the practice of Hippocrates: First, mitigate the pain with fomentation of melilote, mercury, mallows, lintseed, camomile, althea. Then let the womb be prepared with syrup of hyssop, caliment, and mugwort,—In diseases which have their rise from moistness, purge with pills. In effects which are caused by emptiness or dryness purge with a potion. Fasten a cupping glass to the belly, with a great flame, and also the navel, especially if the swelling be flatulent: Make an issue on the inside of each leg, a hand-breadth below the knee.

The air must be hot and dry, moderate exercise is allowed; much sleep is forbidden, she may eat the flesh of partridges, larks, chickens, mountain birds, hares, conies, &c. Let her drink be thin wine.

CHAP. XI.
Of Moles and false Conceptions.

THIS disease is called, by the Greeks, mole, and the cause of this denomination is taken from the load or heavy weight of it, it being a mole, or great lump of hard flesh burdening the womb.

is defined to be an inarticulate piece of flesh, [with]out form, begotten in the matrix, as if it were a conception. In which defination we are to note [two] things. First, in that a mole is said to be in[articu]late, and without form; it differs from mon[sters], which are both formate and articulate. Se[cond]ly, it is said to be as it were a true conception [whic]h puts a difference between a true conception [and a] mole, which difference holds good three ways: [First] in the genus, in that a mole cannot be said to [be an] animal. Secondly, in the species, because it [hath] no human figure, and bears not the character [of a] man. Thirdly, in the individuum, for it hath [no simi]lity with the parent, either in the whole body [or an]y particular of the same.

[Cau]se.] About the cause of this effect amongst [learn]ed authors I find variety of judgments. Some [are o]f opinion, that if the woman's seed goes into [the w]omb, and not the man's; therefore is the mole [prod]uced, others there be that affirm, that it is in[gend]ered of the menstruous blood. But if these two [were] granted, then maids by having their courses [or th]rough nocturnal pollutions, might be subject [to th]e same, which never yet any were. The true [cause] of this fleshy mole proceeds both from the [man] and from the woman; from corrupt and bar[ren s]eed in man, and from the menstruous blood in [the w]oman both mixed together in the cavity of the [wom]b, where nature finding herself weak yet desir[ous] to maintain the perpetuity of her species) la[bours] to bring forth a vicious conception, rather than [none; and so instead of a living creature, generates [a lum]p of flesh.

[Si]gns.] The signs of a mole are these. The [cours]es are suppressed, the appetite is depraved, the [breas]ts swell, the belly is suddenly puffed up, and [wax]eth hard. Thus far the signs of a breeding wo[man], and one that bareth a mole, are all one. I will

shew you how they differ. The first sign of d[ifference]
ence is taken from the motion of a mole, it m[ay be]
felt to move in the womb before the third m[onth]
which the infant cannot; yet the motion cann[ot be]
understood of an intelligent power in the mole[, but]
the faculty of the womb and the feminal spirit[s dif]
fuse through the substance of the mole, for it [is]
not a live animal, but a vegetative in manner [of a]
plant. And secondly, in a mole the belly is sud[den-]
ly puffed up, but in a true conception the be[lly is]
first retracted, and then riseth up by degrees. T[hird-]
ly, the belly being pressed with the hand, the [mole]
gives way, and the hand being taken away, it re[turns]
to the place again; but a child in the womb, th[ough]
pressed with the hand, moves not presently, an[d be-]
ing removed, returns slowly or not at all. L[astly,]
the children continue in the womb not above e[leven]
months; but a mole continues sometimes fo[ur or]
five years, more or less, according as it is fast[ened]
in the matrix. I have known when a mole hat[h fal-]
len away in four or five months.

If it remain until the eleventh month the legs [grow]
feeble, and the whole body consumes, only the [swel-]
ling of the belly still increases; which makes [some]
think they are dropsical, though there be little [rea-]
son for it. For in the dropsy, legs swell and [grow]
big, but in a mole they consume and wither.

Prognostics.] If at the delivery of a mole the [flux]
of the blood be great, it shews the more dange[r, be-]
cause the parts of the nutrition having been vio[lated]
by the flowing back of the superfluous hum[ours,]
where the natural heat is consumed; and then [issu-]
ing with so much of blood, the woman there[by is]
weakened in all her faculties, that she cannot l[ive]
without difficulty.

Cure.] We are taught in the school of H[ippo-]
crates, that phlebotomy causeth abortion; by t[aking]
all that nourishment which should preserve th[e]

of the child. Wherefore, that this vicious conception may be deprived of that vegetive sap by which it lives, open the livre vein and the saphena in both the feet; fasten cupping glasses to the loins and sides of the belly, which done let the uterine parts be first molified, and then the expulsive quality be provoked to expel the burthen.

To laxate the ligature of the mole, take mallows, with the roots three handfuls; camomile, meliloet, pellitory of the wall, violet leaves, mercury, roots of fennel; parsleys of each two handfuls; lintseed, fenugreek, each one pound; boil them in water, and let her sit therein up to the navel. At the going out of the bath, anoint the privities and reins with this unguent following: Take oil of camomile, lillies, sweat almonds, each one ounce; fresh butter labdanum, ammoniac, of each half an ounce; with the oil of lintseed make an unguent.

The air must be tolerably hot and dry, and dry diet, such as do molify and attenuate, she may drink white wine.

CHAP. XII.

Of the Signs of Conception.

IGNORANCE makes women become murderers of the fruit of their own bodies, many having conceived, and thereupon finding themselves out of order, and not knowing rightly the cause, do either run to the shop, of their own conceit, and take what they think fit, or else (as the custom is) they send to the physician for a cure; and he not perceiving the cause of their grief (feeling no certain judgment can be given by the urine) prescribes what he thinks best, perhaps some strong diuretic or cathartic potion, whereby the conception is destroyed. Where fore Hippocrates says, there is a necessity that women should be instructed in the knowledge of conception, that the parent as well as the child might be saved from danger. I will therefore give you some instructions, by which every one may know whether she be with child or not. The signs of conception shall be taken from the woman, from the urine, from the infant, and from experiment.

Signs taken from the woman are these—The first day after conception she feels a light quivering or chilness running through the whole body; a tickling in the womb, a little pain in the lower part of the belly. Ten or twelve days after the head is affected with giddiness, the eyes with dimness of sight: Then follows red pimples in the face, with a blue circle about the eyes, the breast swell and grow hard, with some pain and pricking in them, the belly soon sinketh and riseth again by degrees, with a hardness about the navel. The nipples of the breast grow red, the heart beats inordinately, the natural appetite is dejected, yet she has a longing desire after strange meats; the neck of the womb is retracted, that it can hardly be felt with the finger being put up; and this is an infallible sign. She is suddenly merry, and soon melancholy; the monthly courses are staid without any evident cause; the excrements of the guts are unaccustomedly retained by the womb pressing the great guts, and her desire to Venus is abated.

The surest sign is taken from the infant, which begins to move in the womb the third or fourth month; and that not in the manner of a male, from one side to another, rushing like a stone, but so softly, as may be perceived by applying the hand hot upon the belly.

Signs taken from the urine: The best writers do say that the urine of a woman with child is white, and hath little motes like those in the sun-beams, alcending and defcending in it, a cloud fwimming aloft in an opal colour, the fediments being divided by fhaking the urine, appears like carded wool, the middle of her time the urine turneth yellow, next red, and laftly black, with a red cloud. Signs taken from experience—At night going to bed let her drink water and honey, afterwards if fhe feels a beating pain in her belly and about her navel, fhe hath conceived. Or let her take the juice of cardus, and if fhe vomiteth it up, it is a fign of conception. Caft a clean needle into a woman's urine, put it into a bafon, let it ftand all night, and in the morning if it be coloured with red fpots, fhe hath conceived, but if black or rufty, fhe hath not.

Signs taken from the fex, to fhew whether it be male or female. Being with child of a male, the right breaft fwells firft, the right eye is more lively than the left, her face well coloured, becaufe fuch as the blood is, fuch is the colour; and the male is conceived in purer blood, and more perfect feed than the female; red motes in the urine, fettling down the fediments, foretell that a male is conceived, but if they be white a female. Put the woman's urine which is with child into a glafs bottle, let it ftand clofs ftopped three days, then ftrain it thro' fine cloth, and you will find little living creatures. If they be red it is a male, if white it is a female.— To conclude, the moft certain fign to give credit unto, is the motion of the infant, for the male moves in the third month, and the female in the fourth.

G

CHAP. XIII.
Of untimely Births.

WHEN the fruit of the womb comes forth before the seventh month, (that is, before it comes to maturity) it is said to be abortive, and in effect the children prove abortive, (I mean not alive) if it be born in the eighth month. And why children born in the seventh or ninth month may live, and not in the eighth month, may seem strange, yet it is true; the cause thereof by some is ascribed unto the planet under which the child is born; for every month from the conception to the birth is governed by his proper planet. And in the eighth month Saturn doth predominate, which is cold and dry:—Coldness being an utter enemy to life, destroys the nature of the child. Hippocrates gives a better reason, viz. The infant being every way perfect and complete in the seventh month desires more air and nutriment than it had before; which because he cannot obtain he labours for a passage to go out; and if his spirits became weak and faint, and have no strength sufficient to break the membranes and come forth, as is decreed by nature, that he should continue in the womb till the ninth month, that in that time his wearied spirits might again be strengthened and refreshed; but if he returns to strive again the eighth month, and be born he cannot live, because the day of his birth is either past or to come. For in the eighth month (faith Aven) he is weak and infirm; and therefore being cast into the cold air, his spirits cannot be supported.

Cause.] Untimely birth may be caused by cold, for as it maketh the fruit of the tree to wither and to fall down before it be ripe, so doth it nip the fruit of the womb before it comes to full perfection, and makes it to be abortive; sometimes by humidity, weakening the faculty that the fruit cannot be restrained till the due time. By dryness or emptiness, defrauding the child of its nourishment. By one of these alvine fluxes of phlebotomy and other evacuations: By inflammations of the womb and other sharp diseases. Sometimes it is caused by joy, laughter, anger, and especially fear; for in that the heat forsakes the womb, and runs to the heart for help there, (and so the cold strikes in the matrix, whereby the ligaments are relaxed, and so abortion follows;) wherefore Plato, in his time, commanded that the women should shun all temptations of immoderate joy and pleasure, and likewise avoid all occasions of fear and grief. Abortion also may be caused by the corruption of the air, by filthy odours, and especially by the smell of the snuff of a candle; also by falls, blows, violent exercise, leaping, dancing, &c.

Signs.] Signs of future abortion are extenuation of the breasts, with a flux of watery milk, pain in the womb, heaviness in the head, unusual weariness in the hips and thighs, flowing of the courses. Signs foretelling the fruit to be dead in the womb, are hollowness of the eyes, pain in the head, anguish, horrors, paleness of the face and lips, gnawing of the stomach, no motion of the infant, coldness and looseness of the mouth of the womb, and thickness of the belly, which was above is fallen down, watery and bloody excrements come from the matrix.

CHAP. XIV.

Directions for Breeding Women.

THE prevention of untimely births consist in taking away the aforementioned causes, which must be effected before and after the conception.

Before conception, if the body be over hot, cold, dry, or moist, correct it with the contraries; if cacochmical, purge it; if phlethriocal, open the liver vein; if too gross extenuate it; if too lean, corroborate and nourish it. All diseases of the womb must be removed, as I have shewed.

After conception let the air be temperate, sleep not overmuch, avoid watching, exercise of body, passions of the mind, loud clamours and filthy smells; sweet odours are also to be rejected of those that are hysterical. Abstain from all things that provoke either the urine or courses, also from salt, sharp and windy meats; a moderate diet should be observed.

The couch is another accident which accompanieth breeding women, and puts them in great danger of miscarrying, by a continual distillation falling from the brain. To prevent which, shave away the hair from the cornal and satical coissures, and apply thereon this plaister. Take resinæ half an ounce; laudani one dram; citron peel, lign aloes, olibani, of each one dram; stirachis liquidæ and siccæ a sufficient quantity; dissolve the gums in vinegar, and make a plaister at night going to bed, let her take the fume of these trochisks cast upon the coals.

In breeding women there is a corrupted matter generated, which flowing to the ventricle, dejecteth the appetite, and causeth vomiting. And the stomach being weak, not able to digest this matter, sometimes sends it to the guts, whereby is caused a flax in the belly, which greatly stirreth up the faculty of the womb. To prevent all these dangers, the stomach must be corroborated as follows: Take lign aloes, nutmeg, of each one dram; mace, clove, laudanum, of each two scruples; oil of spike an ounce; musk two grains; oil of mastic, quinces, wormwood, of each half an ounce; make an anguent for the stomach, to be applied before meals.—Another accident which perplexeth a woman with child is swelling of the legs, which happens the first three months by superfluous humours falling down from the stomach and liver; for the cure whereof, take oil of roses two drams; salt, vinegar, of each one dram; shake them together until the salt be dissolved, and anoint the legs hot therewith, chaffing it with the hand: By pursuing it more properly, if it may be done without danger, as it may be in the fourth, fifth, or sixth month of purgation; for the child in the womb is compared to an apple on the tree; the first three months it is weak and tender, subject with the apple to fall away; but afterwards the membranes being strengthened, the fruit remains firmly fastened to the womb, not apt to mischances, and so continues all the seventh month, till growing nearer the time of its maturity, the ligaments are again relaxed, (like an apple that is almost ripe) and grows looser every day until the fixed time of delivery. If therefore the body is in real need of purging, she may do it without danger in the fourth, fifth or sixth month, but not before nor after, unless in some sharp diseases, in which the mother and child both are like to perish.

Apply it to the reins in the winter time, and remove it every twenty-four hours, lest the reins be over hot therewith. In the interim anoint the privities and reins with unguent, confitissæ; but if it be summer-time, and the reins be hot, this plaister following is more proper: Take of red roses one lb; mastick, red sanders, of each two drams, pomegrant peel, prepared coriand. of each two drams and an half; barberries, two scruples; oil of mastick and quinces, of each one ounce; juice of plaintain two drams; with pitch make a plaister; anoint the reins also with unguentum, sandal.

CHAP. XV.

Directions to be observed by Women at the Time of their falling in Labour, in order to their safe Delivery, with Directions for Midwives.

AND thus having given necessary directions for child-bearing women, how to govern themselves during the time of their pregnancy, I shall add what is necessary for them to observe, in order to their delivery.

The time of birth drawing near, let the woman send for a skilful midwife, and that rather too soon than too late; and against which time let her prepare a pallet, bed, or couch near the fire, that the midwife and her assistants may pass round, and help on every side as occasion requires, having a charge of linen ready, and a small stool to rest her feet against, she having more force when they are bowed than when they are otherwise.

Having thus provided, when the woman feels her pain come, and weather not cold, let her walk about the room, resting herself by turns upon the bed, and so expect the coming down of her water, which is a humour contracted in one of the outward membranes, and flows thence when it is broke by the struggling of the child, there being no direct time fixed for the efflux, though generally it flows not above two hours before the birth, motion will likewise cause the womb to open and dilate itself, when lying long in bed will be uneasy, yet if she be very weak, she may take some gentle cordial to refresh herself, if her pain will permit.

If her travail be tedious, she may revive her spirits with taking chicken or mutton broth, or she may take a poached egg, but must take heed of eating to excess.

As for the postures women are delivered in, they are many, some lying in their bed, some sitting in their bed, or chair, some again on their knees, being supported upon their arms; but the most safe and commodious way is in the bed, and then the midwife ought to mind the following rules. Let her lay the woman upon her back, her head a little raised by the help of a pillow, having the like help to support her reins and buttocks, and that her rump may lie high, for if she lies low, she cannot be well delivered. Let her keep her knees and thighs as far distant as she can, her legs bowed together and her buttocks, the soals of her feet and heels being placed on a little log of timber placed for that purpose, that she may strain the stronger: And then to facilitate it, let a woman stroke or press the upper part of the belly gently, and by degrees. Nor must the woman herself be faint-hearted, but of good courage, forcing herself by straining and holding her breath.

In case of delivery, the midwife must wait with patience till the child, or other members, burst the membrane: for if, through ignorance or haste to go to other women, as some have done, the midwife tear the membrane with her nails, she endangers both the woman and the child: For its laying dry, and wanting that slipperiness that should make it easy, it comes forth with great pain.

When the head appears, the midwife must gently hold it between her hands, and draw the child at such time as the woman's pains are upon her, and at no other; slipping by degrees her fore-fingers under his arm-pits, not using a rough hand in drawing it forth, lest by that means the tender infant receive any deformity of body. As soon as the child is taken forth, which is for the most part with its face downwards, let it be laid on its back, that it may more freely receive external respiration, then cut the navel-string about three inches from the body, tying that end which adheres to the belly with a silken string as near as you can, then cover the head and stomach of the child well, suffering nothing to come upon the face.

The child being thus brought forth, and if healthy, lay it by, and let the midwife regard the patient in drawing forth the secundines; and this she may do by wagging and stirring them up and down, and afterwards with a gentle hand drawing them forth: And if the work be difficult let the woman hold salt in her hands, and thereby she will know whether the membranes be broke or not. It may be also known by causing her to strain or vomit, by putting a finger down her throat, or by straining or moving her lower parts, but let all be done out of hand. If this fail, let her take a draught of raw elder-water, or yolk of a new laid egg, and smell to a piece of assafœtida, especially if she be troubled with a windy cholic. If she happen to take cold, it is a great obstruction to the coming down of the secundines, and in such cases the women ought to chaff the woman's belly gently not only to break the wind, but oblige the secundines to come down. —But these proving ineffectual, the midwife must chafer with her hand the extern or orifice of the womb, and gently draw it forth.

CHAP. XVI.

In Case of Extremity, what ought to be observed, especially to Women who in their Travail are attended with a Flux of Blood, Convulsions, and Fits of the Wind.

IF the woman's labour be hard and difficult, greater regard must be then had, than at other times;

and first of all the situation of the womb and posture of lying must be cross the bed, being held by strong persons to prevent her slipping down, or moving herself in the operation of the surgeon: Her thighs must be put asunder, as far distant as may be, and so held; whilst her head must lean upon a bolster, and the reins of her back be supported after the same manner; her rump and buttocks being lifted up, observing to cover her stomach, belly and thighs with warm linen, to keep them from the cold.

The woman being in this posture, let the operator put up his hand, if he find the neck of the womb dilated, and remove the contracted blood that obstructs the passage of the birth; and having by degrees gently made way, let him tenderly move the infant, his hand being first anointed with sweet butter, or a harmless pomatum. And if the waters be not come down, then without difficulty may they be let forth; when, if the infant should attempt to break out with its head foremost, or cross, he may gently turn it to find the feet; which having done, let him draw forth the one and fasten it to a ribbon, then put it up again, and by degrees find the other, bringing them as close and even as may be, and between whiles, let the woman breathe, urging her to strain to help nature to perfect the birth, that he may draw it forth; and the readier to do it, that his hold may be the surer, he must wrap a linen cloth about the child's thighs, observing to bring it into the world with its face downwards.

In case of a flux of blood, if the neck of the womb be open, it must be considered whether the infant or secundine comes first, which the latter sometimes happening to do, stops the mouth of the womb, and hinders the birth, endangering both the woman and the child; but in this case the secundines must be removed by a swift turn; and indeed they have by their so coming down deceived many, who feeling their softness, supposed the womb was not dilated, and by this means the woman and the child, or at least the latter has been lost. The secundines moved, the child must be sought for, and drawn forth, as has been directed; and if in such a case the woman or child die, the midwife or surgeon is blameless, because they did their true endeavour.

If it appears upon enquiry, that the secundines comes first, let the woman be delivered with all convenient expedition, because a great flux of blood will follow, for the veins are opened, and upon this account two things are to be considered.

First, The manner of the secundines advancing, whether it be much or little; if the former, and the head of the child appear first, it may be guided and directed towards the neck of the womb as in the case of natural birth; but if there appear any difficulty in the delivery, the best way is to search for the feet, and thereby draw it forth; but if the latter, the secundine may be put back with a gentle hand, and the child first taken forth.

But if the secundine be far advanced, so that it cannot be put back, and the child follow it close, then are the secundines to be taken forth with much care, as swift as may be, and laid without cutting the entrail that is fastened to them, for thereby you may be guided to the infant, which, whether alive or dead, must be drawn forth by the feet in all haste, though it is not to be acted unless in case of any great necessity, for in other cases the secundines ought to come last.

And in drawing forth a dead child, let these directions be carefully observed by the surgeon, viz, if the child be found dead, its head foremost, delivery will be the more difficult; for it is an apparent sign the woman's strength begins to fail her, and that the child being dead, and wanting its natural force can be no ways assisting to its delivery, wherefore the most certain and safe way for the surgeon, is to put up his left hand, sliding it as hollow in the palm as he can, into the neck of the womb, and into the lower part thereof towards the feet, and then between the head of the infant and the neck of the matrix, when having a hook in the right hand couch it close, and slip it above the left hand, between the head of the child and the flat of the hand, fixing it in the bars of the temple towards the eye; for want of a convenient coming at these in the occiputal-bone, observe still to the left hand in its place, and with it gently moving and stirring the head; and so with the right hand and hook draw the child forward, admonishing the woman to put forth her utmost strength, still drawing when the woman's pangs are upon her; the head being drawn out, with all speed he must slip his hand up under the arm holes of the child, and take it quite out, giving these things to the woman——viz. A toast of fine wheaten bread in a quarter of an ounce of ipocras wine.

If it so happen that any inflammation, swelling, or congealed blood be contracted in the matrix, under the film of these tumours, either before or after the birth, where the matter appears thinner, then let the midwife with a pen-knife or incision instrument launch it, and press out the corruption, healing it with a pessary dipped in oil of red roses.

If at any time through cold, or some violence, the child happen to be swelled in any part, or hath contracted a watery humour; if it remain alive, such means must be used as are least injurious to the child and mother; but if it be dead, that humour must be let out be incision to facilitate the birth.

If (as it often happens) that the child comes with its feet foremost, and the hands dilating themselves from the hips; in such cases the midwife must be provided with necessary ointments to stroke and anoint the infant with, to help its coming forth, lest it turn again into the womb, holding at the same time, both the arms of the infant close to the hips, that so it may issue forth after its manner, but if it proves too big, the womb must be well anointed.— The woman may also take sneezing powder to make her strain: Those who attend may gently stroke her belly to make the birth descend, and keep the birth from retiring back.

And sometimes it falls out that the child coming with the feet foremost, has its arms extended above its head; but the midwife must not receive it so, but put it back again into the womb, unless the passage be extraordinary wide, and then she must anoint the child and the womb; nor is it safe to draw it forth, which may be done in this manner; the woman must be lain on her back, with her head depressed, and her buttocks raised; and the midwife, with a gentle hand, must compress the belly of the woman towards the midwife, by that means to put back the infant, observing to turn the face of the child towards the back of its mother, raising up its thighs and buttocks toward her navel, that so the birth may be more natural.

If a child happens to come forth with one foot, the arm being extended along the side, and the other foot turned backward, then must the woman be instantly brought to her bed, and laid in the posture above described, at which time the midwife must carefully put back the foot so appearing, and the woman rocking herself from one side to the other, till she find the child is turned, but must not alter her posture, nor turn upon her face. After which she may expect her pains, and must have great assistance and cordials to revive and support her spirits.

At other times it happens that the child lies across in the womb, and falls upon its side; in this case the woman must not be urged in her labour, neither can any expect the birth in such a manner; therefore the midwife, when she finds it so, must use great diligence to reduce it to its right form, or at least to such a form in the womb, as may make the delivery possible and more easy, by moving the buttocks, and guiding the head to the passage; and if she be successful herein, let her again try by rocking herself to and fro, and wait with patience till it alter its manner of lying.

Sometimes the child hastens the birth, by expanding its legs and arms; in which as in the former the woman must rock herself, but not with violence, till she finds those parts fall to their proper stations, or it may be done by a gentle compression of the womb, but if neither of them prevail, the midwife with her hand must close the legs of the infant, and if she come at them, do the like to the arms, and so draw it forth; but if it can be reduced of itself, to the posture of a natural birth, it is better.

If the infant comes forward with both knees foremost and the hands hanging down upon the thighs, then must the midwife put both knees upward, till the feet appear; taking hold of which with her left hand, let her keep her right hand on the side of the child, and in that posture endeavor to bring it forth.

But if she cannot do this, then also must the woman rock herself till the child is in a more convenient posture for delivery.

Sometimes it happens, that the child passes forward with one arm stretched on its thighs, and the other raised over its head, and the feet stretched out length in the womb; in such a case the midwife must not attempt to receive the child in that posture, but must lay the woman on the bed, in the manner aforesaid, making a soft and gentle compression on her belly, to oblige the child to retire, which if it does not, then must the midwife thrust it back by the shoulder, and bring the arm that was stretched above the head, to its right station; for there is more danger in these extremities, and therefore the midwife must anoint her hands first, and the womb of the woman with sweet butter, or a proper pomatum, thrusting her hand as near as she can, to the arm of the infant, and bring it to the side.

But if this cannot be done, let the woman be laid on her bed to rest awhile, in which time, perhaps the child may be reduced to a better posture, which the midwife finding, she must draw tenderly the arms close to the hips, and so receive it.

If an infant come with its buttocks foremost, and almost double, then the midwife, anointing her hand must thrust it up, and gently heaving up the buttocks and back, strive to turn the head to the passage, but not too hastily, lest the infant's retiring should shape it worse, and therefore it cannot be turned with the hand, the woman must rock herself on the bed, taking some comfortable things as may support her spirits, till she perceives the child to turn.

If the child's neck be bowed, and it comes forward with its shoulders, as sometimes it doth, with the hand and feet stretched upwards, the midwife must gently move the shoulders, that she may direct the head to the passage; and the better to effect it, the woman must rock herself as aforesaid.

These, and other the like methods are to be observed, in case a woman hath twins, or three children at a birth, as sometimes happens. For as the single birth hath but one natural way, and many unnatural forms, even so it may be in double or treble births.

Wherefore in all such cases, the midwife must take care to receive that first which is nearest the passage, but not letting the other go, lest by retiring it should change the form. And when one is born, she must be speedy in bringing forth the other; and this birth, if it be in the natural way, is more easy, because the children are commonly less than those of a single birth, and so require a lesser passage. But if this birth come unnaturally, it is far more dangerous than the other.

In the birth of twins, let the midwife be very careful that the secundines be naturally brought forth, lest the womb being delivered of its burthen fall, and so the secundines continue longer than is consistent with the woman's safety.

But if one of the twins happen to come with the head, and the other with the feet foremost, then let the midwife deliver the natural birth first, and if she cannot turn the other, draw it out in the posture it presses forward, but if that with its feet downward be foremost, she may deliver that first turning the other side.

But in this case, the midwife must carefully see that it be not a monstruous birth, instead of twins a body with two heads, or two bodies joined together, which she may soon see; if both the heads come foremost, by putting up her hand between them as high as she can, and then if she find they are twins, she may gently put one of them aside to make way for the other, taking the first which is most advanced, having the other, that she do not change its situation.

And for the safety of the first child, as soon as it comes forth out of the womb, the midwife must tie the navel-string as has been before directed, and also bind it with a large and long fillet, that part of the navel that is fastened to the secundines the more ready to find them.

The second infant being born, let the midwife carefully examine whether there be not two secundines, for sometimes it falls out, that by the shortness of the ligaments, it retires back to the prejudice of the woman. Wherefore left the womb should close, it is most expedient to hasten them forth with all convenient speed.

If two infants are joined together by the body as sometimes it monstrously falls out, then though the the heads should come foremost, yet it is convenient if possible to turn them, and draw them forth by the feet, observing that when they come to the hips to draw them out as soon as may be.

And here great care ought to be used in anointing and widening the passage. But these sort of births rarely happen.

CHAP. XVII.
How Child-bearing Women are ordered after Delivery.

IF a woman has had very hard labour, it is necessary she should be wrapt up in a sheep's skin taken off before it is cold, applying the fleshy side to her reins and belly. Or, for want of this, the skin of a hare or coney, flead off as soon as killed, may be applied to the same parts.

Let the woman afterwards be swathed with fine linen cloth, about a quarter of a yard in breadth, chaffing her belly before it is swathed with oil of St. John's wort; after that raise up the matrix with a linen cloth many times folded, then with a little pillow, or quilt, cover her flanks, and place the swathe somewhat above the haunches, winding it pretty stiff, applying at the same time a warm cloth to her nipples, and not presently applying the remedies to keep back the milk, by reason of the body at such a time is out of frame, for there is neither vein nor artery which does not ſtrongly bent, and remedies to drive back the milk being of a diſſolving nature, it is improper to apply them to the breaſts during ſuch diſorder, leſt by ſo doing evil humours be contracted in the breaſt. Wherefore twelve hours at leaſt ought to be allowed for the circulation and ſettlement of the blood, and what was caſt upon the lungs, by the vehement agitation during the labour, to retire to its proper receptacles

She muſt by no means ſleep preſently after delivery, but about four hours after ſhe may take broth, caudle, or ſuch liquid victuals as are nouriſhing; and if ſhe be diſpoſed to ſleep, ſhe may be very ſafely permitted. And this is as much (in caſe of a natural birth) as ought immediately to be done.

If the mother intend to nurſe her own child, ſhe may take ſomething more than ordinary, to increaſe the milk by degrees, which muſt be of no continuance, but drawn either by the child or otherwiſe.— In this caſe likewiſe obſerve, to let her have corriander or fennel-ſeed, boiled in her barley broth, and if no fever trouble her, ſhe may drink now and then a ſmall quantity of white wine or claret.

And after the fear of a fever, or contraction of humour in the breaſt is over, ſhe may be nouriſhed more plentifully with the broath of pullets or veal, &c. which muſt not be till after eight days from the time of her delivery, at which time the womb, unleſs ſome accident hinder, has purged itſelf. It will then be expedient to give cold meats, but let it be ſparing that ſo ſhe may the better gather ſtrength.

And let her, during the time, reſt quietly and free from diſturbance, not ſleeping in the day-time if ſhe can avoid it.

CHAP. XVIII.

How to expel the Cholic from Women in Child-birth.

THESE pains frequently afflict the woman no less than in pains of her labour, and are by the ignorant taken many times the one for the other, and sometimes they happen both at the same instant, which is occasioned by a raw crude, and watery matter in the stomach, contracted through ill digestion, and while such pain continues the woman's travail is retarded.

Therefore to expel such fits of the cholic, take two ounces of oil of sweet almonds, and an ounce of cinnamon water, with three or four drops of the spirit of ginger, then let the woman drink it off.

If the pain prove the gripping of the guts, and long after delivery, then take the root of great comfrey, one dram; nutmeg and peach kernels, of each two scruples, and give them to the woman as she is laid down, in two or three spoonfuls of white wine; but if she be feverish, then let it be in as much of warm broth.

THE
FAMILY PHYSICIAN:

BEING CHOICE AND APPROVED REMEDIES FOR SEVERAL DISTEMPERS INCIDENT TO HUMAN BODIES, &c.

For Apoplexy.

TAKE man's skull prepared, powder of the roots of male-prony, of each an ounce and a half; contrayerva, bastard dittany, angelica, zedoary, of each two drams, mix and make a powder, whereof you may take half a dram, or a dram.

A powder for the epilepsy or falling sickness.

Take of opoponax, crude antimony, dragon's blood, castor penny seeds, of each an equal quantity, make a subtile powder. The dose, from half a dram in black cherry water. Before you take it the stomach must be cleansed with some proper vomit, as that of Mysinct's emetic tartar, from four grains to six. If for children salts of vitriol, from a scruple to half a dram.

A vomit for swimming in the head.

Take cream of tartar half a scruple, castor two grains, mix all together for a vomit, to be taken at four o'clock in the afternoon. At night going to bed it will be very proper to take a dose of apostolic powder.

For an head-ach of long standing.

Take the juice of powder, or distilled water of hoglice, and continue the use of it.

For spitting of blood.

Take conserve of comfrey, and of hipps, of each an ounce and a half; conserve of red roses three ounces; dragon's blood a dram; species of hyacinths two scruples; red coral a dram; mix, and with syrup of red poppies make a soft electuary. Take the quantity of a walnut night and morning.

A powder against vomiting.

Take crabs eyes, red coral, ivory, of each two drams burnt; hartshorn one dram; cinnamon and red saunders, of each half a dram, make a full subtile powder, and take half a dram.

For a looseness.

Take of Venice treacle and diascordium, of each half a dram in warm ale, water-gruel, or what you best like, last at night going to bed.

For the bloody flux.

First take a dram of the powder of rhubarb in a sufficient quantity of the conserve of red roses, early in the morning; then at night take of fortified or roasted rhubarb half a dram, diascordium a dram and a half, liquid laudanum cydoniated a scruple; mix and make a bolus.

For inflammation in the lungs.

Take curious water, ten ounces, water of red poppies three ounces, syrup of poppies an ounce, pearl prepared a dram, make a julep, and take six spoonfuls every fourth hour.

Pills very profitable in an asthma.

Take gum ammoniac and bedellium, dissolved in vinegar, of squills of each half an ounce, powder of the leaves of hedge, mustard, and savoury, of each half a dram, flour of sulphur three drams, and with sufficient quantity of syrup of sulphur make a mass of small pills, three whereof take every evening.

An electuary for the dropsy.

Take choice rhubarb one dram, gum lac prepared two drams; zyloaloes, cinnamon, longbirth-wort of each half an ounce; the best English saffron half a scruple, with syrup of chycory and rhubarb mak an electuary. Take the quantity of a nutmeg, or a small walnut every morning fasting.

For weakness in women.

After a gentle purge or two, take the following decoction, viz. A quarter of a pound of lignum vitæ, sassafras two ounces, raisins of the sun eight ounces, liquorice sliced two ounces; boil all in six quarts of water to a gallon; strain and keep it for use. Take half a pint at four o'clock in the afternoon, the third last at night going to bed.

A clyster proper in a pleurisy.

Take clean French barley a handful; leaves of mallows, mercury, violets, of each a handful and a half; twelve damask prunes; boil all in a sufficient quantity of water to a pint and a half, when strained, add an ounce and a half of fresh cassia and red sugar, with the yolk of an egg. This may be injected every other day.

An ointment for the same.

Take the oil of violets, sweet almonds, of each an ounce, with whey and a little saffron make an ointment; warm it, and bath with it the part affected.

An ointment for the itch.

Take sulphur vive in powder half an ounce, oil of tartar per dilinquium a sufficient quantity, ointment of roses four ounces, make a liniment; to which add a scruple of the oil of rhodium to aromatise it, and rub the part affected with it.

For a running scab.

Take two pounds of tar, incorporate into a thick mass with good sifted ashes, boil the mass in fountain water, adding leaves of ground-ivy, white horehound, fumitory, roots of sharp pointed dock, and of elecampane, of each four handfuls; make a bath to be used, with care of taking cold.

For worms in children.

Take worm seed half a dram; flour of sulphur a dram; sal prunelly half a dram; mix and make a powder. Give as much as will lie on a silver three pence night or morning in treacle or honey. Or for people grown up, you may add a sufficient quantity of aloe rosatum, and so make them up into pills, three or four thereof may be taken every morning.

For the gripes in children.

Give a drop or two of the oil of annifeeds, in a spoonful of panada, milk or what else you think fit.

Of the Judgment of Physiognomy taken from all Parts of the human Body.

HE whose hair is partly curled, and partly hanging down is commonly a wife man or a fool, or else as very a knave as he is a fool. He whose hair groweth thick on his temples and his brow, is by nature simple, vain, luxurious, lustful, credulous, clownish in his speech and conversation. He whose hair is of a redish complexion, is for the most part proud, deceitful, detracting, venerous, and full of envy. He whose hair is very fair, is for the most part a man fit for all praise-worthy actions, a lover of honors, and more inclined to good than evil, careful to perform whatsoever is committed to his care, secret in carrying on any business, and fortunate. Hair of a yellowish colour, shews a man to be good and willing to do any thing, fearful, bashful, weak of body, but strong in the abilities of the mind, and more apt to remember than to revenge an injury.— He whose hair turns grey or hoary, in the time of his youth, is generally given to women, vain, false, unstable and talkative.—*Note,* That whatsoever signification the hair has in men, it is the same in women also.

He whose forehead riseth in a round, signifies a man liberal, of a good understanding inclined to virtue. He whose forehead is very low and little, is of a good understanding, magnanimous but extremely bold and confident, and a pretender to love and honour. He whose **forehead** seems sharp and pointed up in the corners of his temples, is a man naturally vain, fickle and weak in intellectuals. He whose brow is full of wrinkles, and hath as it were a coming down in the middle of his forehead, is one of a great spirit, a great wit, void of deceit, and yet of a hard fortune. He whose forehead is long and high, and jutting forth, is honest, but weak and simple, and of an hard fortune.

Those eye-brows that are much arched, whether in man or woman, and which, by a frequent motion, elevate themselves, shew the person to be proud, high spirited, vain glorious, a lover of beauty, and indifferently inclined to either good or evil. He whose eye-brows are thick, and have but little hair upon them, is weak in his intellectuals, and two credulous.

Great and full eyes, either in man or woman, shew the person to be for the most part slothful, bold, envious, a bad concealer of secrets, miserable, vain, given to lying, and yet of a bad memory, slow of invention, weak of his intellectuals, and yet very much conceited of that little wisdom he thinks himself master of. He whose eyes are hollow in his head, and therefore discerns well at a great distance, is one that is suspicious, proud and treacherous; but he whose eyes are as it were starting out of his head, is a simple foolish person. He who looks studiously and acutely, with his eyes, and eye-lids downwards, it denotes him to be malicious, impious towards God, and false towards men. Those whose eyes are often twinkling, and which move backward and forward, shews the person to be luxurious and unfaithful. If a person has any greenness mingled with the white of their eyes, they are often silly, false and vain. Those whose eyes are addicted to bloodshot, are naturally choleric, perfidious, without shame, much inclined to superstition. They who have eyes like oxen, are persons of good nutriment, but of a weak memory, and of a dull understanding; but those whose eyes are neither two little nor too big, and inclining to black, do signify a man mild, peaceable, honest, witty, and of a good understanding, and one that when need requires will be serviceable to his friend.

A long and thin nose, denotes a man bold, curious and vain, weak and credulous. A long nose, the tip bending down, shews the person to be wise and discreet. A bottle nose denotes a man to be impetuous in obtaining his desires. He who hath a long and large nose, is an admirer of the fair sex, and well accomplished for the wars of Venus, but ignorant of any thing else. A nose very round at the end of it, having but little nostrils, shews the person to be very munificent and liberal, true to his trust, but very proud, credulous and vain. He whose nose is more red than any other part of his face, is thereby denoted to be covetous. A thick nose with wide nostrils, denotes a man dull of apprehension, simple, and a liar.

When the nostrils are close and thin, they denote a man to have but little testicles, and to be very desirous of the enjoyment of women, but modest in his conversation; but he whose nostrils are great and wide, is usually well hung and lustful, but withal of an curious, bold and treacherous disposition, and though dull of understanding yet confident enough.

A great and wide mouth shews the man to be bold, warlike, shameless, and stout, a great liar, and as great a talker and carrier of news, and also a great eater, but as for his intellectuals they are very dull.

The lips when they are very big and blubbering,

shew a person to be credulous, foolish, dull and stupid, and apt to be enticed to any thing.

When the teeth are small, and but weak in performing their office, and especially if they are short and few, though they shew the party to be of a weak constitution, yet they denote him to be of an extraordinary understanding, and not only so, but also of a meek disposition, honest, faithful and secret in whatever they are trusted with.

A tongue too swift in speech shews a man to be very foolish and vain. A stammering tongue signifies a weak understanding, and of a wavering mind. A very thick and rough tongue denotes a man to be apprehensive, full of compliments, yet treacherous and prone to impiety.

A faint voice, attended with little breath, shews a person to be of good understanding but timerous.

A thick full chin, abounding with peace, honest and true to his trust. A picked chin shews one to be of a lofty spirit.

Young mens beards usually begin to grow on their chins at fifteen years of age, and sooner; these hairs proceed from the superfluity of heat, the fumes whereof ascend to the chin and cheeks, like smock to the funnel of a chimney; there are few women that have hair on their chins, and the reason is, those humours which cause hair to grow on mens cheeks are evacuated by women in their monthly courses.

Great thick ears are certain signs of a foolish person, of a bad memory, and worse understanding; but small and thin ears shews a person to be of good wit and understanding, grave, secret, thrifty, modest, of a good memory, and willing to oblige.

A face apt to sweat on every occasion, shews the person to be of a hot constitution, vain and luxurious, of a good stomach, but of a bad understanding, and worse conversation. A lean face shews a man

H

to be both bold in speech and action, but withal foolish and deceitful. A face every way of due proportion, denotes an ingenious person, one fit for any thing, and much inclined to what is good.

General Observations worthy of Note.

WHEN you find a red man to be faithful, a tall man to be wise, a fat man to be swift on foot, a lean man to be a fool, a handsome man to be proud, a poor man not to be envious, a knave to be no liar, an upright man not too bold and hearty to his own loss; one that drawls when he speaks, not to be crafty and circumventing; one that winks on another with his eyes, not to be false and deceitful; a sailor and a hangman to be pitiful, a poor man to build churches, a quack doctor to have a good conscience, a bailiff not to be a merciless villain, an hostess not to over-reckon you, and an userer to be charitable: Then say you have found a prodigy, and men acting contrary to the common course of their nature.

FINIS.

www.ingramcontent.com/pod-product-compliance
Lightning Source LLC
Chambersburg PA
CBHW022136160426
43197CB00009B/1303